MW01028388

LAGOON TIME

LAGOON TIME

A Guide to Gray Whales
and the
Natural History of San Ignacio Lagoon

by
Steven L. Swartz

THE OCEAN FOUNDATION

Lagoon Time by Steven Swartz, Ph.D.
A Project of The Ocean Foundation

Published by The Ocean Foundation
Produced by A Higher Porpoise Design Group
        Pieter A. Folkens, Designer, Editor, Illustrator

Copyright © 2014 Steven L. Swartz
Photographs by Steven L. Swartz unless otherwise indicated. Additional photographs
and images copyright by the various credited sources. Used by permission.
Printed version *Lagoon Time* ISBN: 978-0-916251-42-0
eBook version *Lagoon Time* ISBN: 978-0-916251-43-7

All rights reserved under International and Pan-American Copyright Conventions.
Published in the United States of America.

First Edition Published January 2014

Distributed by:
Sunbelt Publications, Inc.
P.O. Box 191126
San Diego, CA 92159-1126
(619) 258-4911, fax: (619) 258-4916
www.sunbeltbooks.com

18 17 16 15 14   5 4 3 2 1

Lagoon Time, A Guide to Gray Whales and the Natural History of San Ignacio Lagoon
written and photographed by Steven L. Swartz. — 1st ed.

Dedication

I WISH TO DEDICATE this book to some very special people in my life. First is my lifelong sweetheart Mary Lou Jones, widely known as "Lulu." Her love, companionship, and friendship are but a few of the qualities that have made her the love of my life. We share so many things, including the thrill of adventure and discovery of things in the wild. We spent our early days together at Laguna San Ignacio, and she knows full well the immensity of the lagoon's spirit and its influence on our lives then, now, and ever after.

Next is Mike G. Symons who first introduced Mary Lou and I to the wonders of Baja California. With his keen interest and sense of humor in all things, Mike made sure that we lived every day to the fullest.

Then there are Francisco "Pachico" Mayoral and his wife Carmine. Pachico first to show us the lagoon in its entirety; Carmine provided wisdom for the soul with her words and strength for the body with her tortillas: the best in all of Baja California.

Finally, I thank those colleagues throughout Mexico and elsewhere who share the belief that we are obligated to maintain wild places like Laguna San Ignacio to provide a balance to our developed world. Through such actions we demonstrate that local communities can prosper, while preserving and conserving wilderness areas and wildlife. By so doing they enrich their lives, the lives of their children, and the lives of visitors from all over the world, and thus ensure gray whales and other species of marine life will always have Laguna San Ignacio as their home.

Contents

PART II   A Guide

Laguna San Ignacio Ecosystem Science Program

The Laguna San Ignacio Ecosystem Science Program (LSIESP) vision is for an ecologically robust marine protected area that hosts sustained, low-impact, environmentally friendly eco-tourism and fishing operations for the economic and social benefit of the local communities, Mexico, and to benefit the wildlife that depend on this unique coastal marine ecosystem. It is the MISSION of the program to develop and implement a sustained ecosystem based science program that provides wildlife and land managers, and the local community with information on the status and trends of the Laguna San Ignacio ecosystem, addresses complex ecosystem issues at scales appropriate to management questions, and that recognizes the natural and human-related mechanisms affecting the ecosystem. Such information is fundamental to evaluate conservation alternatives and options, and to assess the outcome of management and conservation measures implemented to determine if they achieve their intended purposes.
See more at: http://www.lsiecosystem.org

The Ocean Foundation

The Ocean Foundation (TOF) is a unique community foundation with a mission to support, strengthen, and promote those organizations dedicated to reversing the trend of destruction of ocean environments around the world.

Our vision is to:
• To protect and restore oceans around the world
• To steer human interaction with the ocean and coasts toward a sustainable future by building a strong, vibrant and well-connected community of donors, grantees and projects that effectively responds to urgent issues and seizes on key opportunities for global marine conservation
• To provide leadership to the ocean conservation community — working together, achieving a better understanding of the threats to the marine environment (as well as solutions) along with stronger capacity and effectiveness
See more at: http://www.oceanfdn.org/about

Publication of *Lagoon Time* was made possible by the generous contributions and advance adoption by the American Cetacean Society, Los Angeles Chapter; Baja Discovery, Inc.; Philanthropiece; Searcher Natural History Tours; Spirit of Adventure Charters; The Marisla Foundation; and The Ocean Foundation.

Foreword

GRAY WHALES MAKE one of the longest migrations of any mammal on earth. Every year they swim over 10,000 miles round trip between Mexico's nursery lagoons and feeding grounds in the Arctic.

One of my early major marine conservation campaigns was to help with the protection of Laguna San Ignacio in Baja California Sur, one of the primary gray whale breeding and nursery lagoons—and still, I believe, one of the most beautiful places on earth. In the late 1980's, Mitsubishi proposed establishing a huge salt works in the lagoon and surrounding areas. The Mexican government was inclined to approve this industrial development for economic development reasons, despite the fact that the lagoon already had multiple designations as a protected area both nationally and internationally.

A determined five-year campaign formed and drew upon thousands of donors who supported an international effort that was implemented by a partnership that included many organizations. Movie stars and famous musicians joined with local activists and American campaigners to stop the salt works and bring international attention to the plight of the gray whale. On Thursday, March 2, 2000, Mexico's then-President Ernesto Zedillo announced that he had decided to cancel, and Mitsubishi Corporation had agreed not to pursue, the Laguna San Ignacio salt works. We had won!

The Laguna San Ignacio campaign remains one of the best case studies of the challenges and successes of cross-border, cross-sectoral, and cross-disciplinary collaboration; one that used the rule of law in Mexico to hold the state and its representatives accountable to their constituencies.

In February 2010, a group of aging activists, their friends, and families gathered in Laguna San Ignacio to celebrate the 10th anniversary of the victory of this hard fought campaign to protect the great gray whale nursery for future generations to enjoy. As we celebrated with a cake there at the lagoon, gathered were familiar faces with whom we had spent many long hours in conference rooms, in courtrooms, and thankfully, here at the lagoon. Among our families and friends, the victory was one of the signature stories of their lives, just as the campaign had bonded an odd group of activists—local, regional, national, and international—into a campaign team who shared an unforgettable experience.

Because of those stories, my stepdaughter had asked to turn 18 with the whales, joining me on this trip to celebrate. Like so many visitors, she learned the joy of riding out to the whales in the pangas, the swift rush of hand against wet whale skin as they rose to be patted, and the quiet evenings spent watching the sunset and telling stories under the thatched roof.

As part of that 10th anniversary gathering at one of the rustic camps of Laguna San Ignacio, we took the children of the local community out on their first ever whale-watching expedition in the pangas. While this is the activity that provides the winter livelihood for their families, the children had never been—gas was too costly and the opportunity never arose. Their smiling faces made the day a special memory.

Our group included campaigners such as Joel Reynolds of NRDC who still works on behalf of marine mammals every day, and Jared Blumenfeld, who has gone on to serve the environment in government service. Also among us was the late Patricia Martinez, one of the conservation leaders in Baja California whose commitment and drive carried her places she could not have imagined in defense of that beautiful lagoon. We traveled to Morocco and Japan, among other places, to defend the Lagoon's World Heritage status and ensure global recognition for the threats it faced. Patricia, her sister Laura, and other community representatives were a major part of our success and remain a continuing presence in defense of other threatened places along the Baja California peninsula.

When the campaign started, the lagoon was already a designated UNESCO World Heritage Site. In addition, Laguna San Ignacio, lays within the boundaries of Latin America's largest biosphere reserve, "El Vizcaíno," formed by presidential decree in 1988 to protect, among other resources, gray whales because of its use by gray whales to spend the winters and calve their young. In short, the salt works project was incompatible with the area's land-use zoning, its tri-level biosphere reserve, World Heritage Site, and Mexican Sanctuary status provisions, and their intended conservation objectives.

I remember my first visit to the Lagoon in 1995. I was down there to look at the landscape, talk to the local people, and gain first hand knowledge of what was at stake. During the five years of the campaign, I went back many times—in January when the big males were there, in February and March as the calves began to arrive, and in April when the last of the whales started their long migration north.

The story of the gray whale nursery of Laguna San Ignacio is story of protection supported by vigilance and enforcement. It is the story of local, regional, and international cooperation. And, it is the story of working out the differences to achieve a common goal.

We know there have been changes at the lagoon, and will be more changes in the future. We can hope that most of those changes are for the good of the whales and the small human communities who depend on them—and for the lucky visitors who get to see these magnificent creatures up close and carry their own signature story away. And I hope that the memories will serve as a reminder to remain supportive and vigilant to ensure that the gray whale success story remains a success story.

ABOUT THIS BOOK

This book is a special creative project of The Ocean Foundation. As such, Lagoon Time is a popular, first-hand account of the experiences and amazing discoveries made by Dr. Steven Swartz, Mary Lou Jones, and their colleagues regarding the life history of gray whales, the international conservation efforts that halted the development of a destructive salt works on the shores of the lagoon by a large multinational corporation, and the local community's efforts to ensure that this unique marine ecosystem will survive the inevitable tide of development.

This book provides the visitor, the thousands of previous visitors and whale watching enthusiasts from around the world an accurate look into the human and natural history of Laguna San Ignacio, as well as a handy field guide to gray whale behavior and the diverse botanical and avian wildlife in the area. The intent of the book is to provide the visitor to the lagoon with an orientation guide of sorts; to the things they will see and experience once they arrive at the lagoon, especially the gray whales and what the science programs there are telling us about the whales, and other wildlife that call the lagoon and adjoining estuary system home. And, Steven was fortunate to enlist the help of Pieter Folkens, a marine illustrator of international recognition, to design the book and to contribute his expertise the project.

All of this is presented in the context of Mary Lou Jones and Steven Swartz's early experiences exploring the lagoon years ago, starting the scientific investigations at the lagoon from 1977-1982, which set the stage for the eventual "Ecosystem Science Program" that began in 2006 in partnership with Dr. Jorge Urban R. Also included is the early history of the 19th century whalers that put the gray whale breeding lagoons on the map, the development of the biosphere reserve, the threat of the salt plant development, then the social and economic development of the area, and finally the re-establishment of a science program to report on the health of the lagoon and its flora and fauna.

The proceeds from the sales of this book will provide on-going financial support for the research and conservation efforts of this Laguna San Ignacio Ecosystem Science Program, A project of The Ocean Foundation.

— Mark J. Spalding

Prologue

A FRIEND AND FELLOW whale aficionado Roger Payne once told me that he looked forward to the next stage in the development of our relationship with whales, hopefully one of mutual respect for each other's co-existence. For a brief moment in time we found and lived that "next stage" at a personal level on the shores and waters of Laguna San Ignacio. Others followed. They came and continue to come from all points on the globe to visit and experience the lagoon and the gray whales. The scientific findings of our field studies in Laguna San Ignacio were used, in part, by the Mexican government as the basis for developing whale watching guidelines and establishing protected areas for whales within the lagoon. During the late 1990s threats of the industrialization of Laguna San Ignacio spawned "salt wars" over the proposed building of an industrial scale solar salt production facility within the lagoon and its surrounding desert. The public outcry in opposition to such a development clearly demonstrated that modern society was developing an appreciation for balance between industrial development and preservation of wilderness, and a willingness to pay the price of co-existence with wild areas and the non-humans that occupy them.

For us, our days at La Laguna and our experiences there forever changed our lives and attitudes about wilderness, conservation, and appreciation of who we are. Getting there, however, was not exactly a walk in the park. And once there, well, as National Geographic film Producer Nick Noxin put it "My God, we might as well be going to Africa!"

Islas San
Benitos

Laguna
Guerrero
Negro

Isla de
Cedros

Laguna
Ojo de Liebre

Bahía de Ballenas

Laguna
San Igancio

Bahía
Topolobampo

Bahía Navitsche

Bahía
de Altata

Bahía Magdalena

Cabo San Lucas

Introduction

The Beginning

*The wilderness, rough, harsh, and inexorable, has charms more potent in
their seductive influence than all the lures of luxury and sloth, and often
he on whom it has cast its magic finds no heart to dissolve the spell, and
remains a wanderer and an Ishmaelite to the hour of his death.*
— Francis Parkman

PUNTA PIEDRA (also known as Rocky Point), is a low, flat projection of sand-
stone and shell-rock jutting out into Laguna San Ignacio, Baja California
Sur, Mexico. It was our home each winter from 1977 until 1982. There Mary
Lou and I lived with the gray whales that seasonally occupied the lagoon.

It was late January in 1977 when we first walked along the shores of Laguna San Ignacio. Our primary objective was to document the gray whales that
utilized the lagoon during the winter months to birth and care for their newborn calves, and breed to ensure the survival of the species going forward. We
carefully noted the whales' weekly abundance and distribution, the number of
human visitors to the lagoon, all the while documenting the lagoon and it's
wildlife. At the time we had no idea how those winters we spent camped at the
lagoon would affect our future, shape our ideals for conservation of wild areas,
and underscore the importance of Baja's lagoon habitats so critically necessary
for the gray whales' survival.

What experiences we had there—the tears cried out of joy and of sadness,
the people we met, and the whales that allowed us to live among them. There
I listened to the wind for the first time. Now I often just sit and listen to the
sounds of the wind and it awakens memories of those times. The cackle of a raven or the distant chorusing of coyotes trigger thoughts, images, and sensations
that I first experienced on those shores. No more spectacular or inspiring a view
exists than the Sierra de Santa Clara as seen from Punta Piedra at dawn or dusk,
or watching desert dust storms sweeping down from the mesas to overtake the

(*Opposite*) The Baja California Peninsula noting bays and lagoons mentioned in the text.
Image: Aqua satellite, Jacques Descloitres, MODIS Rapid Response Team, NASA/GSFC.

lagoon's waters. The plunge of an osprey plucking a fish from the depths, or a gray whale calf learning to breach and discovering life above the water's surface. Returning to life outside the lagoon each year, the daily routine of home in San Diego, paled in its apparent significance. Yet it was because of life outside the lagoon we went back, and why we must continue to visit. It is life outside the lagoon that creates a longing for and a very real need to experience and appreciate such wild places. And therein is a responsibility to ensure that such places are maintained, lest a little more of the human spirit dies.

While many things have changed at Laguna San Ignacio since that time, one of the most impressive things is all that has remained the same; a sort of universal constant that wild places like the lagoon and the surrounding Baja desert preserve for all time. Laguna San Ignacio is one of those truly unique places that remains timeless. Native Indian societies that camped along its shores in pre-historic times depicted the lagoon's marine animals in their cave paintings and petroglyphs high in the Sierra de San Francisco, to the east of the lagoon. Yankee whalers, most notable Captain Charles M. Scammon, came to plunder the gray whales, but also noted the unique features of the lagoon and its wildlife in his logbooks and drawings. Today's modern day eco-tourists also experience a majestic array of marine organisms that flourish in the productive coastal waters and contrasting stark harshness of the surrounding desert; an environment that remains as it always has been, serene yet dramatic in its richness and depth.

Despite the changes in human habitation, the lagoon's features, the constancy of lunar driven tides and cyclic winds continue to leave their impressions on the lives of those that come to visit now and in the future. It is this consistency that is perhaps the most enduring and endearing feature of the place. Most impressive to the visitor is the diverse variety of coastal and marine animals that call Laguna San Ignacio their home for all or a part of each year. The world is fortunate that the human residents of Laguna San Ignacio and the government of Mexico have seen fit to make this area a federally protected marine sanctuary, and thereby ensure that it will persist for generations of people to visit and appreciate. But it wasn't always like that . . .

"Lagoon Time"

At Christmas each year beginning in 1977 we found ourselves embattled among holiday shoppers as we prepared for three months of camping in a remote portion of the southern Baja desert. At a time when most families draw together, we were focused on leaving town. Frantically we searched for necessary camping gear and other essential items, made countless arrangements for coordinating our field season from afar, and waited for our research grants to arrive. Funding, like the beginning of the whale season, came at the end of the year. So, as soon as the check arrived, we would begin a shopping spree of true holiday proportions. Coleman stoves and lanterns, wind proof tents, water proofing, inflatable boats and outboard motors, crates of batteries, 35mm film, audio tapes, ice coolers, and more all had to be gobbled up before the holiday shoppers grabbed the last remaining items. Too often we heard apologetic merchants say "you should have been here a week ago, I had dozens of them, but now I am sold out."

Ultimately we would cross off the last remaining items on our seemingly endless lists of things to do, load our vehicles, and venture across the border from San Diego into Mexico. Our route took us through Tijuana, past the seaside bull ring to Ensenada, then south to Santo Tomás, and finally found us slip-

Mary Lou, Pero Pinto, Radar, and Mike Symons on the road to Laguna San Ignacio in 1978.

Mary Lou and Steven on Punta Piedra in 1977.

ping into rural Baja California. Past the dry lake Laguna Chapala, the boulder pile, stopping for lunch at El Rosario or Santa Inez for a look at a painted cave. Reaching the statue of the eagle in the center of the highway at the 28th parallel and the town of Guerrero Negro, marked the border between the states of Northern and Southern Baja California, and signaled that we were less than a day from our destination.

In those days it took at least two days to get to the town of San Ignacio, even longer if the winter rains had recently washed out portions of the highway. There was only one, Baja No. 1. It crossed a number of arroyos that habitually flooded with the winter rains. When stopped for gas or for a rest during these first few travel days, except for our voices, we heard a ringing sound in our ears - the inertia from the sounds of the city that we lived with most of the days of our lives. But ever so slowly, day by day, the ringing would subside and yield to the domineering silence of the desert. The ringing was replaced by the sound of sand under your feet as you walked, a Kangaroo-rat in the brush, the "cackle" of a raven perched on a Cardón cactus, the screech of an osprey overhead with a fish in its talons, or the squeaking of cormorants wings as they flew up the lagoon to roost for the night. And most memorable perhaps, the blows of the whales across the water on still nights. These were the predominant sounds at La Laguna.

Eager to get started each year, we wanted to do everything at once. Set up camp, begin surveying the lagoon's growing whale population, see what had changed from the previous year. But there was always something in the way- the wind, the tide, a broken spring on the truck, and so on. Slowly and with some frustration, we relinquished control of the pace of our actions. We settled into the rhythm and dictates of a new timekeeper that would ultimately control all our activities. Carefully planned schedules of weekly whale counts, surveys, and countless environmental measurements all yielded to the bidding of the winds and tides. The days of the week gave way to the phase of the moon. Schedule what you wish, but if the wind was to blow or the tide was running the wrong direction, you just waited for the next opportunity and found something else to do in the meantime. Somehow the essential tasks were always accomplished and, in the end, it seems that we accomplished even more than we ever expected.

The visitor to the lagoon must resign himself to the pace of the winds, the tides, and in doing so, all the wonder of the place becomes accessible. This annual transition in attitude and perception, a slowing of daily life to follow more natural clocks, developing a full appreciation of what each day brought us, for better or worse, is what we came to call "Lagoon Time."

Why Gray Whales and Why San Ignacio?

It is hardly necessary to say, that any person taking up the study of marine mammals, and especially the cetaceans, enters a difficult field of research, since the opportunities for observing the habits of these animals under favorable conditions are but rare and brief. My own experience has proved that observation for months, and even years, may be required before a single fact in regard to their habits can be obtained.
— Charles M. Scammon 1874

In the mid-1970s wintertime whale watching was becoming a popular pastime in San Diego. Gray whales could be viewed during their annual southward migration from just about any location along the coast. Organizations like the San Diego Natural History Museum and the American Cetacean Society sponsored local excursions to see the whales, as well as week long trips to see the whales in their breeding lagoons along the Pacific Coast of Baja California. Natural historians like Dr. Raymond Gilmore pioneered these excursions aboard chartered sport-fishing vessels that carried up to two dozen whale-watchers. Once inside the lagoons, small skiffs were launched to take the passengers around to view the whales. Such excursions, particularly to the remote Laguna San Ignacio, raised concerns that U.S. citizens may be violating the recently passed Marine Mammal Protection Act by harassing the breeding gray whales, which at that time were listed in the United States as an endangered species.

Mary Lou and I were interested in finding out more about gray whales and their interactions with whale watchers within their breeding lagoons. I held a position as a Research Associate with the San Diego Society for Natural History, Dr. Gilmore's parent institution. In January 1976 at Ray's invitation we attended a meeting at his home in La Jolla to discuss the status of gray whales in Baja California. Both he and Dr. Carl Hubbs of Scripps Institution of Oceanography had documented the slow recovery of the Eastern North Pacific population of gray whales, and had flown surveys over the breeding lagoons in the 1950s and 1960s to document the whales' return to their historical breeding grounds. That day, we all met with William Samaras and Hazel Sayers of the American Cetacean Society, who had recently returned from a gray whale conference in Baja California. They told us of rumors that the Mexican government had been approached by whaling interests to resume the harvesting of whales in Mexican waters.

Then there were the new concerns that well meaning whale-watchers from the United States might be disturbing the whales in their breeding lagoons. Dr.

Skiffs used by the San Diego based whale-watching boats in the 1980's

Hubbs noted that the current numbers of whales using the lagoons in winter was not well known and needed to be investigated and documented. Thus began our plans to organize a field expedition that we hoped would obtain reliable information on the whales' use of Laguna San Ignacio as a winter breeding area, and information on the activities of the whale-watchers that went to see them.

Within days of our La Jolla discussions Drs. Gilmore and Hubbs arranged a meeting with the Director of the San Diego Natural History Museum, retired U.S. Navy Admiral Davies. Our proposal to visit the lagoons and to assess the status of gray whales there was well received by the Museum's Board of Directors, who agreed to endorse and sponsor our request to the U.S. Marine Mammal Commission for funding to support the study. The Commission had previously sponsored a contract report by Dr. Randy Reeves that raised the issue of uncertainty of the status of the whales in their breeding lagoons, and concern for the potential adverse effects of whale-watching tourism on the whales during their calving period. The Commission agreed to provide a small grant to support an initial site visit to Laguna San Ignacio in 1977. To this, Dr. Hubbs and his wife Laura contributed matching funds. With this assurance, planning for the trip began in earnest.

Shortly after New Years 1977 we found ourselves driving my fully packed VW van down the Baja Hwy No.1. Carl and Laura Hubbs, and Ray Gilmore had briefed us on the lagoons in the months before we departed. They generously

A gray whale in a "tail-up headstand" in Laguna San Ignacio.

provided their notes, advice and shared their observations from many years of visits to Baja California. Ray gave us copies of his hand drawn charts of Laguna San Ignacio that he based on those of Captain Charles M. Scammon dating from 1874, along with a 1907 survey of the lagoon by the U.S. Hydrographic Office. Much of the lagoon's interior was left to the imagination as Ray admitted he had never seen the entire interior. He instructed us in the use of the Brunton Compass and charged us with surveying the entire lagoon interior and drawing an accurate map.

The winter of 1977 was largely a reconnaissance, a pilot study to gather sufficient information to see what really needed to be done to determine what was going on in the lagoon and how best to do it. Our report of the 1977 season to the Marine Mammal Commission included recommendations for a five year program that would gather baseline information on the whales' use of the lagoon and document the visitation of the area by whale watchers. From this, we proposed, the status of the whales and their use of this area could be reliably discerned. Mr. John Twiss and Dr. Robert Hofman, then the Executive Director and Scientific Program Director, respectively, of the Marine Mammal

Commission listened carefully to my descriptions and observations of the wintertime activities in Laguna San Ignacio when I met with them the summer following our first visit to the lagoon. The scope of the research program that we proposed, however, was beyond the means of the Commission, but they agreed to help in whatever way they could. They arranged for me to meet with Mr. Buff Bohlen, then with the World Wildlife Fund while I was in Washington, DC. He listened to my accounts of the lagoon, and asked many questions. He seemed interested, supportive, but non-committal. When we parted he told me he would take our proposal to their Research Board for consideration and that we should hear from them in a few weeks. A few weeks passed. We heard from World Wildlife; we were to return to the lagoon in 1978 with specific research plans, adequate funding, equipment, and more staff.

We were fortunate to hear from many supporters over the project's five years. Individuals, public and private organizations responded to our requests for funding with their contributions of financial support, equipment, and time. National Geographic loaned us their Avon inflatable boat when we lost ours. The following year, the Avon Corporation custom built one to our specifications and then donated it to the project. Mercury Outboard Motors, Inc. saw that each year we had outboard motors in good operating condition. The whale watching boats from the San Diego sport fishing landings arranged to transport our gear and supplies to the lagoon, making the otherwise intimidating logistics manageable. The Mexican government provided the necessary permits to conduct the research in their country.

Local support came from the fishermen and their families in Laguna San Ignacio. They were always there for us with advice, help, and freely shared their lifelong experience and knowledge of the lagoon and the whales. Our first year they thought we were tourists. When we returned the second year speaking a little more Spanish, they thought we were still tourists, just persistent. By year three, we were attending potluck dinners at their homes and meeting their families. By years four and five we had become semi-permanent fixtures in the neighborhood and on a first name basis with many of the local families. We shared interests in the local issues, and freely discussed the state of the local fishing industry and the well being of the lagoon's resources. In the lagoon everyone communicated by CB radio, which is better than telephone because it is on all the time. We rallied to each other's aid during storms, gas and water shortages, or when someone's return from a day of fishing was overdue. Despite our eccentric scientific activities, "la comunidad de San Ignacio" always showed us their warmth, hospitality and friendship becoming of true "Californianos." Privately, they later confided to us, they did wonder why we preferred to live in tents out on windswept Punta Piedra (Rocky Point) rather than build a house farther up the lagoon.

Rolling Down Baja 1

On our first trip down the Baja 1 highway in January 1977 we were accompanied by Robert and Shirley, a couple who worked for Baja Frontier Outfitters. They had been to the lagoon before and would provide our initial logistical support. Also along were two wildlife photographers under the employ of National Geographic Magazine. Bill Weaver and Ken Nelson were on assignment to photograph the recently reported "friendly" gray whales for a National Geographic television special on whales and whale researchers produced by Nick Noxin. The previous year the San Diego newspapers reported that some gray whales had begun to approach whale watching boats in Laguna San Ignacio, and in some instances allowed whale watchers to "pet" them. We never doubted that we would see lots of gray whales, but would we encounter these "friendly whales"? Would the National Geographic team capture this new phenomenon on film? All this and more swirled through our minds as we passed through the city of Ensenada and into the Santo Tomás valley.

As we made our way further and further south we read to each other from

Eagle monument at the 28th Parallel

The beginning of the 60 km road from town to Laguna San Ignacio.

Tom Miller's "Baja Book," which at the time was the most reliable source of information for travelers venturing into Southern Baja California. It was an innovative travel guide because it overlaid the highway and other roads on early satellite photographs of the Baja peninsula. In addition to driving directions, it was annotated with bits of natural history of the peninsula's fauna and flora, historical notes and bits of local lore and points of interest. After crossing the mesas, boulder fields, and the "Boojum" trees (*Fouquieria columnaris*, or Cirio) of the Cataviña region, we descended into the Vizcaíno Desert plane. Here the highway runs as straight as a chalk line snapped on the desert floor. Out of the mirage appeared the metal sculpture of an eagle, marking the 28th parallel, the town of Guerrero Negro and the border between northern and southern Baja California. The town of San Ignacio was a mere half day drive further down the highway.

As you approach from the north, you really cannot see San Ignacio from the highway. The town of two thousand or more residents is located in an oasis of lush palms and citrus orchards tucked in a valley where the vast Vizcaíno Desert meets the foothills of the Sierra de San Francisco to the east. The town is located in a canyon or arroyo eroded over millennia by an underground freshwater river that comes to the surface to form an oasis.

When we entered the town of San Ignacio for the first time in the winter of 1977 we found sprawling bay trees in the town center. Under the shade taxi cab drivers polished their cars and talked with locals about local things. Ranchers drove by in their pickups wearing their wide brimmed cowboy hats. School children in crisp uniforms were strolling through the square sipping on sodas and laughing. The sound of chickens crowing was everywhere and many seem to roam the town oblivious to the constant stream of traffic in the dusty street. On the northeast corner stood the "Super Mercado" owned and operated by Sr. Manuel Meza. We found it to be a substantial general store offering local fruits and vegetables, car parts, clothing, hats, and just about everything else one would ever require. In fact, as Sr. Meza informed us, "If you don't see what you need, let me know and I will get it for you." Right now cold beer was in order. And of course, some local information on the best route from town to the lagoon.

According to Sr. Meza, the most reliable route was a few miles back up the highway to the north, and marked by an old house foundation and low rock wall. Following a delightful lunch of chicken tacos at a local café, and topping off our gas and water tanks at the PEMEX station, we set off to find "El Camino de La Laguna."

The author visits Sr. Meza in 2011, many years after their first encounter.

1 The Backstory

Crystal Bluff: Those That Came Before

FROM TIME TO TIME I've visited locations that held the presence of previous human occupation. "Crystal Bluff" or "Cantil Cristal" is such a place. It held a special significance for us and, judging from the numerous ancient shell middens there, it was a popular location with early pre-historic lagoon residents as well. Approaching the bluff from the lagoon you first encounter a field of rock pinnacles 2–3 m high and sculpted by the wind and waves into smooth, convoluted, and surreal shapes. Walking to the base of the bluff and while scaling its sides to reach the top, each of us always felt as if we were visiting someone's camp or home — a "presence" filled the air. We named the bluff for the gypsum crystals that ran in veins along its face. We were told that geologic forces related to volcanism deep below the desert had caused this piece of sandstone to rise some 30 m higher relative to the lagoon shore as the surrounding alluvial basin sank around it.

Cantil Cristal (Crystal Bluff)

Approximately one km long, Cantil Cristal faces the islands to the east in the northern lagoon basin. We have no idea how long it had been there, but it was obvious that its height offered a vista of the surrounding desert that would be of strategic advantage to any group wishing to keep sentinel around their camp.

As we explored its slopes for the first time one day in January 1977 we marveled at the vista of the entire lagoon from its summit. We soon learned that we were not the first to walk these slopes. As we worked our way down the southern side of the bluff I heard Lulu scream out. I hurried in her direction expecting to find her fallen down the slope, bitten by a snake, or something awful. As I approached, she extended her hand, in which was an exquisite, perfectly shaped black obsidian spear-point covering almost her entire palm.

We were in someone's previous home. Layers and layers of shells, some a meter or more deep in places, flanked Cantil Cristal on its north and south sides. These middens are evidence of earlier, prolonged human activity at this site. In every direction along the slope were fragments of black obsidian glass, finished, unfinished, and broken projectile points, broken basalt scrapers, and other rocks that had been worked into primitive tools.

To the west we could see a large sand dune and the bend in the lagoon that marked the lower channels that led to breaking surf that defined its entrance to the open ocean beyond. To the north were the Sierra de Santa Clara, the remnants of a massive ancient volcano system. To the south were extensive mangrove marshes along the southern shore of the lagoon, and beyond that, dry lakes that shimmered white with salt accumulated over the centuries.

We surmised that this was an obvious place for a camp, as its altitude allowed residents to see who was coming or going from any direction. The contents of the shell middens clearly indicated that shellfish were abundant, as would have been flounder, sting rays and other fish in shallows, as there are today. Ancient peoples would likely visit these coastal lagoons to collect salt and seafood, and the evidence all around us indicated this campsite was a favorite that had been used extensively over time. Now, as we watched a mother and calf gray whale move up into the northern basin of the lagoon, we wondered what those ancient people thought of these immense animals that visited the lagoon during the winter. Were they also curious about the whales? Did they hunt them?

Harry Crosby, an expert on Baja California history, has written a book about cave paintings of Baja California. He noted that there were pictures of marine creatures, including whales and dolphins, painted on and petroglyphs chipped into the stone cliffs and walls of caves in the Sierra de San Francisco many kilometers east of the lagoon, but not far from the town of San Ignacio. The ancient inhabitants may have traveled west from the mountains to the shore, perhaps making records of their winter observations of whales while foraging around the lagoon. The mountain caves may have been secretive religious sites, or used seasonally to avoid colder winter temperatures, or as a refuge from summer heat in the lowlands. It is also possible that the lagoon's shores were closer then.

Several features in this pictograph are enough to conclude it contain a depiction of
a whale, but what activity does the human figure next to the whale represent? What
are in his hands? This shaman-like figure is quite similar to depictions of a person over
a dead deer found on the rock walls of many caves in the Sierras east of the lagoon.
Photo: Jeff Foott

Pictographs of large game and shaman-like human figures. Photo: Jeff Foott

The Sierra de San Francisco and Sierra de Guadalupe to the south and east are well known for the pre-contact cave paintings at more than 600 sites tucked deep inside its canyons and steep arroyo walls. In his book on the cave paintings, Crosby noted a depiction of a supernova that occurred in AD 1054. From this and additional anthropological evidence, he concluded that the great murals and other cave paintings date from AD 500 to 1300.

Crosby's dating is consistent with a period known as the Medieval Climate Optimum (AD 950–1250) when cultures flourished in many places around the globe, including the North American Southwest. Weather in the region is believed to have been somewhat wetter then, with more abundant vegetation. Alan Watchman, a geoscientist at the Australian National University and his colleagues have been conducting research on similar rock art in Sierra de Guadalupe since 2001. They have dated some of the expressions back as far as 7,500 years ago, to periods that include several Holocene Climate Optimums. These hypsithermals (warming periods) led to sea levels greater than 3 m higher than present due to winter temperatures warming 3° to 9°C in some places.

Looking at the San Ignacio region from space, one can see outlines of previous lagoon shores reaching much farther east than now. It is also easy to see the course of a river that once flowed down the arroyo past the present-day town of San Ignacio into an alluvial fan of silt at the edge of the ancient lagoon.

These revelations of geology, archaeology, and climatology invite us to imagine the presence of the whales way back then. The gray whale's primary feeding area in the Arctic had been ice-free for hundreds, if not thousands of years. Recent genetic-based research by Dr. Elizabeth Alter estimating an optimum population size of gray whales suggested the maximum population in the North Pacific Basin may have reached 76,000 to 118,000 individuals. Now they number a little more than 21,000. Could it have been that an ice-free Arctic and lagoons three or four times more extensive than now supported a whale population three to five times greater than now? It makes one wonder.

Anthropologists also wonder what happened to the rock artisans. The only aboriginal inhabitants of central Baja California identified so far are the Cochimí people — a simple culture comprising small autonomous bands of hunter-gatherers. Very few details exist about the Cochimí or their origins other than that their language is related to the Yuman languages farther north and into western

A view from space shows the present-day Laguna San Ignacio in proximity to Crystal Bluff and the Cochimí habitation site of Kadakaamán (present town of San Ignacio). Photo: NASA/Goddard MODIS apparatus on the Aqua satellite.

Arizona. The Cochimí left no evidence of agriculture or metallurgy. The craft of pottery may have reached the northern Cochimí by the time of first contact with Europeans, but it did not reach the area near the lagoons.

A Cochimí settlement known as Kadakaamán (Arroyo of the Carrizos) existed when the first Spanish Missionary arrived at the oasis that eventually became Mission San Ignacio in 1706. Journal entries by the Missionaries documented conversations with the Cochimí who told of pictographs created by a race of giants who lived long before. This was based on the observation that many of the human figures depicted were much taller and pictographs appeared high off the ground. Researchers, including Harry Crosby and Enrique Hambleton, speculate that a different group of early inhabitants predated the Cochimí.

The dates assigned to the latest pictographs coincide with the climate's transition from the Medieval Climate Optimum to the Little Ice Age, when declining temperatures and lower sea levels occurred globally. Across the globe, human populations contracted twenty to over thirty percent over the period, due principally to starvation and disease. Anasazi Pueblos in the southwest and Mayan cities in the Yucatan were abandoned while the Norse settlements in eastern Canada and Greenland failed. At no time since the first rock art was created in Baja Sierras 7,500 years ago had the global climate been so harsh on such a scale. Colder, dryer seasons accompanied by receding lagoon shorelines and expanding deserts made life more difficult for the inhabitants of central Baja California. The simple life of the early culture left few clues beyond the extensive rock art going back millennia. A gap exists in our understanding of the indigenous peoples until the Missionaries first encountered the Cochimí more than three hundred years ago. Perhaps the Cochimí were the surviving descendants of the prolific artisans who left their work on the rocks in the mountains.

Suffice it to say, evidence of ancient human encampments are found at several sites in the area. Their ancient campsites around the shores of Laguna San Ignacio are marked by "middens" containing mounds of shells, stone artifacts and tools, and projectile points and knives manufactured from black volcanic obsidian glass and red jasper brought from the mountains. We can surmise that these people traveled seasonally from the mountains in the east to the coastal lagoons and foraged for the abundant fish, shell fish, turtles, seals, and sea lions, that could be found along the lagoon's shores, and hunted for game across the region.

Their knowledge of whales and other forms of marine life is documented in pre-historic painting and petroglyphs that adorn caves and rock faces in the Sierras to the east of the lagoons. While they presumably had knowledge of gray whales, there is no direct evidence they actively hunted large whales as did the native cultures of the Pacific Northwest and the North Slope of Alaska. However, it is likely that they consumed stranded whales as windfall supplements to their diet, especially young calves that wash ashore each winter.

A February rain in 1979 brought out numerous wildflowers on Crystal Bluff and the surrounding desert.

We would return to Cantil Cristal many times in the years that followed to count whales in the upper lagoon from its summit. We often sat atop the bluff without speaking for prolonged periods. Sitting in the silence, listening to the wind's songs, and looking out over the desert, imagining a prehistoric family camped below, collecting shellfish, marveling at the seasonal appearance of the whales.

Following a series of torrential rains in February 1979, the bluff's dusty brown complexion was transformed into colorful fields of blue lupine, yellow sunflowers, orange poppies, and blue daisies. The wind carried the fragrance of millions of flowers across the bluff to the desert and mudflats below. The flowers brought the insects, and they brought all manner of birds. Now, returned to its dusty dry brown, the only permanent residents were the great horned owls and ravens that nested along the bluff's face. We would always feel a comfortable reverence for this place, and for those that came there before us. We felt somehow connected, and remained respectful visitors.

The Founding of Mission San Ignacio Kadakaamán

While searching for suitable mission sites, Jesuit Francesco María Piccolo came across a reliable fresh water source and the Cochimí settlement of Kadakaamán in 1706 (dated 1716 by some). Two decades later, in 1728, Father Juan Bautista de Luyando founded Misión San Ignacio Kadakaamán, dedicating it to Saint Ignatius of Loyola, founder of the Society of Jesus (Jesuits). It was the thirteenth mission established in Baja California along the "El Camino Real" or "Royal Highway" that spanned most of both Alta and Baja California, from Mission San Francisco Solano de Sonoma north of San Francisco Bay to San Jose del Cabo Añuiti near the southern tip of Baja California.

Friar Fernando Consag initiated construction of the main sanctuary, but it was not completed until 1786 by Dominican Friar Juan Crisóstomo Gómez. He expanded the original structure, using local volcanic stones to enhance the walls that measure four feet thick in places. It was his masonry craft that has allowed this structure to survive nearly 250 years, compared with the adobe walls of many other Missions along the El Camino Real.

Mission San Ignacio settled in the arroyo surrounded by the palm oasis. (1978).

The original (ca. 1786) carved wood doors of Mission San Ignacio Kadakaamán. The main doorway is capped by an ornamental Moorish arch, above which is a relief medallion of the Dominican insignia — an eight-pointed cross with fleurs-de-lis.
Photo: from *Las Misiones Antiguas* by Edward W. Vernon.

The ornate gilded "anástilo retablo" and alter can be seen in the eastern nave of Mission San Ignacio Kadakaamán. The statue in the middle is of St Ignatius Loyola, the founder of the Jesuit society for whom the mission was named. Photo: from *Las Misiones Antiguas* by Edward W. Vernon.

The facade of Mission San Ignacio Kadakaamán.

Over the years, the plentiful and reliable supply of water in the San Ignacio oasis supported the cultivation of numerous types of plants and trees. The
Jesuits planted the distinctive groves of date palms that now dominate the local landscape and provide some income for many of the local inhabitants. The
Jesuits also engineered a water system that channels fresh water from the lake
into the town's stone reservoirs. The 280 year old system remains in use today,
bringing fresh water to the entire community of around 700 inhabitants.

By the late 1760s, epidemics of bubonic plague, small pox, typhus, measles,
and various venereal diseases brought by Europeans and to which the Cochimí
had no immunities wiped out nine of every ten indigenous persons. The Mission
was formally abandoned in 1840 and fell into disrepair. It remained neglected
until the 1970s when it was restored to its present condition, including the original, carved wood doors and gilded alter. But the people it was built to serve did
not survive. The Cochimí language hasn't been spoken since the 1800s and the
Cochimí people no longer exist as a distinct culture, though the Kumeyaay resid-
ing at San Ignacio are occasionally referred to as "Cochimís" by other Mexicans.

Today's visitor will find the stately and well preserved mission and school
buildings presiding over the town square surrounded by shops and houses, an
example of a classic "colonial era" peninsular community.

Captain Scammon and the 19th Century Whalers

Raymond Gilmore told a story about the time he was working as a U.S. Fish and Wildlife Service inspector at the Point Mollate whaling station in Richmond, California in the 1950s. He had met a young woman working as the receptionist at the hotel where he had a room in at that time. When he explained the nature of his work she remarked, "I bet you would be very interested in seeing the contents of my grandfather's sea chest sometime." Her name was Mildred Scammon Decker, the granddaughter of Captain Charles Melville Scammon, the best known of the 19th century's west coast whalers. And yes, Ray did visit the Decker household and found inside Captain Scammon's sea chest a cache of log books, drawings of whaling sites and equipment, and notes on the natural history of the gray whales that Scammon pursued in the lagoons of Baja California and elsewhere. Shortly thereafter, Ray contacted the Bancroft Library at the University of California in Berkeley suggesting they take a kind interest in Mrs. Decker. Eventually Captain Scammon's personal papers were placed into a special collection to be curated and preserved for posterity.

Scammon was born in Pittston, Maine, in 1825 to Eliakim P. Scammon, a Methodist preacher and prominent member of the community. The family's roots are among the earliest English settlers in the Colonies, having arrived in Boston around 1630. Charles was well-read and expressed himself in writing and drawing from an early age. Although certainly a Yankee from a prominent maritime region of New England, he never intended to become a whaler.

Young Scammon's first attempt to ship out to sea came at the age of fifteen years old, but his father would have nothing of it. At seventeen and disregarding his father's desire that he attend college, he signed on as an apprentice seaman with Captain Robert Murray of Bath, Maine, twenty-five miles down the Kennebec River from his home. Within six years he had accepted his first commission to sail the 120-ton schooner *Phoenix* in the merchant trade along the Atlantic seaboard. He also married Susan Crowell Norris. The year was 1848.

In January, James Marshall had found gold in the tailrace of Sutter's Mill in Coloma, California. Though not the first time gold was discovered in the region, this find indicated the precious metal was more common across the state. President James Polk's message to Congress later that year turned gold fever into an epidemic. Commercial cooperatives were formed in New England to build, purchase, and charter ships to transport would be prospectors the treacherous seventeen-thousand nautical miles around Cape Horn to California.

By that time, whaling in the North Atlantic had declined significantly and Yankee whaling companies had already been shifting efforts into the Pacific. Plans developed to take gold seekers "around the Horn" with the expectation that they would commence Pacific whaling after delivering the passengers.

However, upon arriving in San Francisco, entire crews, including captains, abandoned their ships to pursue gold in the foothills of the Sierra Nevada.

Early in 1849 and responding to the demand for sea captains with any experience, twenty-four year old Charles Scammon was asked to refit for passengers the relatively new, 221-ton three-masted bark *Sarah Moers*. He was to ready her for an assignment that would take him to places he had never been before, both geographically and professionally. *Sarah Moers* departed Bath on 26 August 1849. The long assignment would separate Charles from his pregnant wife, but such was the life of a seaman. At less than one hundred feet long (including bowsprit), *Sarah Moers*, her cargo, and passengers made the voyage in 186 days, arriving at San Francisco on 21 February 1850. They found a busy port with a score of ships arriving each day. While many ships arrived, few departed, particularly any returning to the east coast.

Yerba Buena Cove had become cluttered with hundreds of ships at anchor, laying unkempt with no crew and no future. Opportunities for a dedicated sea captain were rare. Scammon endured long periods ashore seeking the next chance to apply his maritime skills. Nearly three months after arriving in California he secured a short run to Oregon for lumber with *Sarah Moers*. He took two more assignments—one on the 200-ton bark *Emma* delivering supplies up the Columbia river and another aboard the bark *J. R. Thompson* for a general cargo and trading venture bound for Valparaiso, Chile. A chance meeting with the Revenue Cutter *Lawrence* in Valparaiso planted a seed in his soul that would eventually dominate his maritime career.

A daguerreotype of abandoned ships in Yerba Buena Cove (San Francisco, winter of 1849–1850) where Scammon anchored *Sarah Moers* in early 1850. Photo: Historic American Buildings Survey, Library of Congress, Prints and Photographs Division.

A daguerreotype panorama of Yerba Buena Cove (San Francisco) in 1851, a year following Scammon's arrival. Photo: Graves Pictoral Collection, Bancroft Library.

He would return from these voyages to find San Francisco looking quite different each time, with more abandoned ships cluttering Yerba Buena Cove. Yet with every assignment he gained valuable knowledge of the Pacific coasts of North, Central, and South America that would play an important role in his future. However, by early autumn of 1851, Charles was out of a job and broke.

In 1852 and compelled by economic necessity, Scammon reluctantly took command of the eighty-foot, 160-ton brig *Mary Ellen* on a "sealing, sea-elephant and whaling voyage" for the Harrington & Ludlow Company. He had never engaged in such activities before and this kind of venture was certainly not his preference, but facing the prospect of having to abandon his profession, he had little choice. The five-month assignment did take him back to sea for his fifth command, but he didn't go far. His crew took elephant seals from Point Reyes just north of the Golden Gate, and may have ventured south to the upper coast of Baja California. No whales were taken on that voyage, only seals and sea lions, but the commercial success of the venture led to a subsequent offer.

His second whaling voyage commenced in November aboard the bark *Rio Grande*. Still largely inexperienced at whaling and with a crew consisting of even less experienced and some totally "green" members, his initial efforts were unremarkable. He decided to work south, hoping to find the valuable sperm whale.

When meeting each other at sea, whaling and merchant ships would gather together in "gams" to exchange mail, news, and information on whales and whaling grounds. The term referred to a social aggregation of whales and was applied equally for social visits among whalers. From such meetings, Scammon gained tips and reports of sightings.

Rio Grande reached Ecuador where the crew secured a large sperm whale. The venture took mostly humpback whales (particularly off Costa Rica and Mexico) and a few other sperm whales. On the last leg of the voyage and to ensure at least a modicum of success, they stopped at East San Benito Island to take what elephant seals they could. Being mid-summer, there were no gray whales around. Leaving two longboats to pursue seals, *Rio Grande* headed for the southeast end of Cedros Island fifteen miles away for fresh water and wood for the tryworks. The near-shore stream became known as Whaler's Spring. Scammon would visit the place several times during the next decade.

Rio Grande returned to port in September and Scammon learned that Susan wanted to join him. He took another coastal commission aboard the small schooner *Mary Taylor* as Susan and four year old Charley traveled south, then north to get west. Just weeks after his family's arrival, the Captain was offered a more lucrative commission to take the full-rig 370-ton ship *Leonore* to China for ship chandler Tubbs & Company. Having earned their sea legs "around the Horn," Susan and Charley joined Charles on the cruise.

Lenore had been part of the Forty-niner invasion, but served only as a storage facility since her arrival. Brothers Alfred L. and Hiram Tubbs refurbished the vessel and encouraged Scammon to sell her in China since there was no shortage of ships available at bargain prices in San Francisco. Although unable to sell *Lenore*, Scammon did secure profitable cargo for a return voyage plus 169 passengers, arriving at San Francisco on 24 March 1855. Then things changed for Captain Scammon.

Whalers and sealers had been calling on Yerba Buena for decades prior to 1848 (the year Alta California became a US territory and the pueblo was renamed San Francisco). Although impacted by the Gold Rush, at least two whalers continued to base operations out of San Francisco. A shift of prominence from New Bedford and the Atlantic fishery to San Francisco and the Pacific grounds had begun when the former New Bedford whaler *Russell* switched registry to San Francisco in 1851.

The whalers in the Pacific typically worked in the higher latitudes seeking sperm, humpback, bowhead, and right whales, all of which were slow swimmers and within the range of oar-powered whaleboats. As autumn turned to winter and like the whales, they left the dark and stormy northern seas, focusing their attentions south. In the early 1800s many crews wintered over at the Sandwich Islands (Hawaii). Honolulu and Lahaina became important way points for provisioning and transshipping (the process of moving product to another vessel for transport, allowing a whaler to stay longer on the grounds). Other whalers continued a winter hunt along the coast from California to South America. One such voyage opened the history of gray whaling in Mexico when Captain John Locke in command of the British whaler *Resolution* crewed by "Nantucketeers" left the northern grounds to take whales off Mexico during the winter of 1795. The crew's backstory provides a historical link to the Atlantic gray whale.

In the mid-seventeenth century, English settlers of Nantucket Island had pursued the "scrag whale" (Atlantic gray whale) from shore, thus beginning the renowned Nantucket whale fishery. Many Nantucketeers remained Loyalists during the American Revolution and, following the War, some Nantucket families emigrated to England. Using British ships crewed by Nantucketeers, British whaling companies transported supplies to the convict colony of Australia, then worked the Pacific whaling grounds. Meanwhile, the three hundred year old rivalry between England and Spain in the New World was being worked out in Nootka Sound (Vancouver Island). In addition to avoiding war between the two Kingdoms, the Nootka Conventions gave British whalers unfettered access to Spanish shores in the west for whaling as Spain was not a whaling nation. *Resolution* was free to work the waters of Baja California. There Nantucketeers found the scrag whale they had taken from the shores of the western Atlantic in previous decades. Locke's crew took a few scrag whales, though they preferred humpback and sperm whales because they yielded more oil for the effort. This was the first known commercial exploitation of gray whales in the Pacific.

Fifty years later in the winter of 1845–1846 and a decade before Scammon's refit of *Lenore*, Captain Joshua Stevens of the Stonington bark *United States* and James Smith in command of the New London ship *Hibernia* became the first Yankee ships to pursue whales in Marguerita Bay (Bahia Magdalena). They also recognized the whales that dominated the bay as the scrag whale known in the Atlantic. Word of the bay's whales eventually reached San Francisco, but the scrag whale was less valuable than others. However, California's population was growing and demand for whale oil increased. By the early 1850s, shore stations in Monterey and elsewhere began taking gray whales to serve the demand.

As chandlers supplying ships out of San Francisco, Tubbs & Company had heard about Magdalena Bay. Although not having sponsored a whaling venture before, the Tubbs brothers saw an opportunity in Captain Scammon's experience and their ship. Immediately upon Scammon's return from China, Tubbs asked him to outfit *Lenore* for whaling and take her along the California coast for anything he could find that yielded oil. Within three weeks following his return, Scammon was off to Baja California on his third whaling voyage.

He returned to Isla Cedros and went as far south as Bahia Magdalena, perhaps to investigate the area for a future foray, as it was summertime and no gray whales were present. They did take humpback whales, pilot whales, and more seals along the coast. This unusually short voyage lasted only a few months. He may have learned of the seasonality of the whales in Bahia Magdalena because he left San Francisco again in December, heading directly to Bahia Magdalena, where his legendary and inextricable connection with the gray whale began.

The schooner *Hopewell* (another Tubbs & Company vessel) rendezvoused with *Lenore* that December. Two other vessels—the brigs *Francis* and *Sarah Mc-Farlane*—were also there. They focused on Bahia Magdalena, the waters around Cabo San Lucas, and Bahia de Ballenas (just north of the entrance to Laguna San Ignacio). The assault on gray whales was now in earnest. This was the beginning of what historian David Henderson described as the "bonanza period" of gray whaling that lasted until 1864–1865. Henderson estimated that 1500 gray whales were killed in the Bahia Magdalena region alone during this period.

Captain Charles Melville
Scammon in his Revenue
Cutter Service Uniform
(*circa* mid-1860s).

The 1855–1856 winter voyage was sufficiently successful that in just two months Scammon transshipped more than four hundred barrels of oil on a northbound ship from Cabo San Lucas so he could remain on the grounds until July. Scammon returned to Magdalena Bay the winter of 1856–1857, again for Tubbs & Company, with the 180-ton brig *Boston* (half the size of *Lenore*, but less expensive to operate as it had one less mast). A shore-based tryworks was built next to the whalers' camps near the small Mexican settlement. As gray whales became scarce there, Scammon and the others began to explore elsewhere along the coast searching for concentrations of gray whales.

During his visits to Whaler's Spring on Isla Cedros, Scammon met and talked with native fishermen who provided information on the presence of marine life that interested him. It is likely that Scammon learned about the lagoons and the whales that migrated there each winter in this way.

The indigenous people and Spanish explorers of Baja California certainly knew of lagoons along the peninsula's Pacific coast. Beginning in the mid-1500s, Spaniards, often with local guides, scouted the Pacific coast for suitable ports for Galleons traversing the Pacific from Asia to Acapulco where goods were transported overland to Veracruz and forwarded on to Spain aboard West Indies Galleons. The Pacific leg of the route utilized favorable currents at around 40°N, but Acapulco was 23° farther south and east. A safe harbor where Galleons could provision and repair near where the current met the continent was immensely desirable, but they determined the lagoons were too shallow and treacherous for consideration as ports.

During an expedition in 1751, Padre Fernando Consag visited a large lagoon (likely Laguna Ojo de Liebre). He noted (as informed by his guides) that whales were frequently seen along the outer coast and inside the lagoon. Later expeditions reported that inhabitants of Isla Cedros built rafts to travel between the island and the peninsula. They apparently hunted pilot whales, dolphins, and seals to supplement their diet. Other explorers also reported whales near the entrances of coastal lagoons, such as Bahia Ballenas, Bahia Vizcaino, and around Isla Cedros, but whaling did not interest the Spaniards. They used tallow instead of whale oil. Marine mammals (with the significant exception of sea otters and fur seals) were not valued the way they were elsewhere in the world.

Whalers were also wary of the waves breaking over the shallow entrances to the lagoons and completely avoided them, not realizing what lay up the lagoon. Apparently what Scammon learned that spring in 1857 made him curious enough to consider checking more closely the lagoons southeast of Isla Cedros that opened into Bahia Vizcaino. He made plans to change strategy at the end of the disappointing summer cruise of 1857. He wrote:

> *We would have been obliged to return to port with nearly an empty vessel, had not nearly all the men volunteered to engage for the winter season, rather than leave the vessel penniless.*

His plan was part ingenious and part clandestine. He wrote to his employer requesting a smallish tender for crossing the dangerous sandbars at the mouth of the lagoons. A.L.Tubbs wanted to discuss the plan in person when Scammon returned home. Rather than tacking *Boston* against the prevailing north-westerlies back to San Francisco, he disembarked at Santa Barbara with Susan and three of his crew, continuing on to San Francisco aboard a steamer. He instructed his first mate to tuck *Boston* into a cove on Santa Catalina in the Channel Islands and wait there while making repairs and preparations.

Tubbs presented Scammon with the small schooner *Marin*, which he outfitted with more tools and supplies. He headed south with Susan and a fresh crew. They rendezvoused with *Boston* in November and soon headed south to Bahia Vizcaino, arriving the first week of December, 1857.

From a favored anchoring spot known as Lagoon Head just inside Morro Santo Domingo, he explored two unnamed lagoons that would eventually become known as Laguna Guerrero Negro and Laguna Manuela (named after the whaling barks *Black Warrior* and *Manuella* that went aground at those entrances). Farther south, *Marin* scouted the entrance to the then-unnamed larger

A drawing of a whaling scene in the Baja California lagoons by Charles Scammon.

"lower lagoon" of Laguna Ojo de Liebre (Eye of the Hare Lagoon, also known as "Scammon's Lagoon"). A few days later, one of the whaleboats returned to *Boston* reporting that *Marin* had safely entered the lagoon and enough water ran over the bar for *Boston* to cross. *Boston* weighted anchor and began to move through the shallow entrance between sandbars.

Then the wind died, leaving the vessel adrift.

Lyndall Baker Landauer delivers a fascinating and detailed telling of the first days of *Boston* trying to enter the lagoon, the near failure of the entire enterprise, and the venture being rescued by a few Kanakas (Hawaiians) on the crew who resorted to surf-boards to save the day. The story appears in her published doctoral dissertation *Beyond the Lagoon: A Biography of Charles Melville Scammon*. It is a highly recommended read for the gray whale enthusiast.

Suffice it to say, the boats eventually made it into the inner lagoon, but the work that lay ahead was difficult and perilous. The crew began to hunt gray whales which were found in abundance. Immediately the operations took a turn as the men learned firsthand of the gray whales' ferocious defensive behavior. The first whale they pursued busted their whaleboat, severely injuring several of crew. Another whale turned the first rescue boat into kindling. It was not to be a unique event. When struck by the lances and harpoons, the injured whales would go after the whaleboats and stove them in, overturning the boats, and seriously injuring the men. The whalers quickly learned that this species did not give up its life easily. Scammon wrote of the pursuit of these "devilfish":

> Hardly a day passes but there is upsetting or staving of boats, the crews receiving bruises, cuts, and, in many instances, having limbs broken; and repeated accidents have happened in which men have been instantly killed, or received mortal injury . . . Hence, these dangerous gray whales were given names like "Devilfish" and "hardhead" in addition to "mussel digger" for the whales' habit of dredging bottom sediments.

Scammon's crew quickly became shy about the whales in the lagoon. Many were too badly injured to man the whaleboats. To counter the danger and avoid further injury and damage, they developed a special style of "lagoon whaling" that involved anchoring a whaleboat in shallow water adjacent to a narrow, but deeper channel. A whale passing by was shot with a lance from a harpoon gun or a "bomb-lance" fired from a small canon, and then finally dispatched from the safety of the shallows as the crew remained out of reach of "the angered animals." The technique was so successful that he planned to leave the lagoon early as they could stow no more oil. However, it took a week of tricky maneuvering to get back across the bar. After stopping at Isla Cedros for water, they returned to San Francisco chock-full of oil. Scammon wrote:

> . . . the vessel so deeply laden that her scuppers were washed by the rippling tide. Thus ended a voyage which in no small degree was a novel one.

Scammon named the area "Boston Lagoon" and returned the following year (1858–1859) with the 300-ton bark *Ocean Bird* and schooners *A. M. Simpson* and *Kate*. More ships participated including Scammon's brother-in-law, Jared Poole,

Etching by Zinco y van de Castelle in *Marine Mammals of the Northwestern Coast of North America* based on Scammon's sketch of using the bomb-lance in San Ignacio Lagoon.

in command of the 200-ton bark *Sarah Warren*, with whom he had an acrimonious relationship The season was another complete success, except for *Ocean Bird* running aground and getting suck on a sand bar for eight days. Scammon was now in his prime as a whaler. His incredible skill as a mariner and tenacity as a whaler brought him recognition. However, Dr. Landauer commented in her biography of Scammon, "He deplored the bloodiness and brutality of whaling and sympathized with the dying whale."

Boston Lagoon became crowed with eleven other ships the winter of 1859–1860. Captain Poole recalled seeing what might be another lagoon while whaling at Bahia de Ballenas. He and Scammon decided to leave to search for it. They found an entrance not much more than two fathoms deep and against a wicked current. They guided their vessels, including the smaller *Carib* and tenders *Kate* and *Nevada,* across the bars and through the breakers to enter Laguna San Ignacio. Two large Yankee ships, *Henry Kneeland* and *John Howland*, had been shadowing Scammon and tried to follow him into the lagoon. One succeeded while the other chose to remain outside the lagoon, sending whaleboats through the breakers and towing a catch back to the main ship. A shore station was established in the upper lagoon. A small ranch on the southern shore bears the name "La Freidera" (The Tryworks) where harvested whales were rendered. Today an eco-tourism company operates whale watching excursions from that location.

Poole and Scammon returned to Boston Lagoon the next winter. Six Yankee whalers also arrived. However, the damage to the whale population was clearly evident. The number of whales was low, as was the yield of oil. Scammon obtained only 245 barrels of oil (seven whales' worth). He would never return to Boston Lagoon. Captain Poole had gone solo in 1861, venturing to bays of mainland Mexico (Reforma, Topolobampo, and Navachiste). However, he lost his ship going aground at Bahía de Altata in 1865. Lagoon whaling continued after 1865, including a visit from the famous whaling ship *Charles W. Morgan*, but the bonanza period of whaling for gray whales was over.

Civil war broke out in the spring of 1861. Captain Scammon enlisted in the US Revenue Marine/Revenue Cutter Service (forerunner of the US Coast Guard), but he had to wait for a commission. Again for economic reasons, Scammon worked two more whaling cruises for Tubbs & Company. That spring he took the 400-ton full-rigged Yankee whaling ship *William C. Nye* north into Russian waters of the Sea of Okhotsk and Shantar Bay seeking bowhead whales. He was able to take only three whales. The cruise was more valuable to him as a future Revenue Cutter Captain than for the oil and whalebone they acquired. He visited Laguna San Ignacio and Bahía Magdalena once more in the winter of 1862–1863. Then Tubbs & Company quit the whaling business and Captain Scammon received his first command in the Revenue Cutter Service.

The gray whale fishery endured into the 1870s, after which catches declined so significantly that the Baja whaling grounds were completely abandoned. Numerous shore whaling stations had appeared along the coast of the California's, but most of them were gone too. Because of their low cost of operations, some persisted, surviving on low catch numbers. Some vessel-based whaling continued to take gray whales along the coast without any regard for conservation, moving on when whales were hard to find. To this Scammon wrote in 1874:

> *The mammoth bones of the California gray lie bleaching on the shores of those silvery waters, and are scattered along the broken coasts, from Siberia to the Gulf of California; and ere long it may be questioned whether this mammal will not be numbered among the extinct species of the Pacific.*

Scammon is best known as a whaler—not something he was proud of—even though the commercial whaling endeavors occupied less than eight years of his fifty-three year career as a mariner, thirty of which spent in the US Revenue Marine. He pursued whales out of an economic necessity, but he was perhaps more fascinated by the adventure of sailing to new and unexplored locations, and learning about the species he and his crews pursued. He was a complex man drawn to the study of natural history, a keen observer, and self-taught scientist. His life long career at sea demonstrated an incredible strength of character, but also unveiled his vulnerability as a human being.

To his credit, his writings and drawings on whales and other marine life enriched the scientific community at a time when the oceans and their creatures were far more mysterious and unknown. While pursuing great whales and other marine mammals at sea, Scammon studied their natural history and biology, taking voluminous notes in journals and logbooks, and making detailed drawings. Articles on his travels became published in newspapers and magazines, including seventeen articles for the *Overland Monthly* magazine beginning in 1869.

His most notable literary accomplishment was the publication in 1874 of *Marine Mammals of the North-West Coast of North America* that included *An Account of The American Whale Fishery*. While in Laguna San Ignacio, Captain Scammon had taken note of the whales' behavior and natural history in detailed writings and drawings. He depicted the characteristic red-mangrove

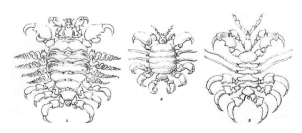

Three of Scammon's scientific illustrations of parasites found on whales. Number 1 in this figure is of the parasitic cyamid crustacean *Cyamus scammoni* described by W. H. Dall.

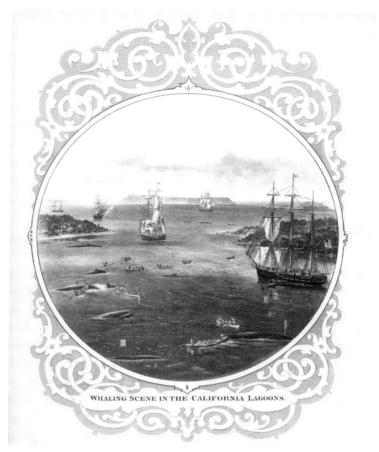

WHALING SCENE IN THE CALIFORNIA LAGOONS.

Captain Scammon's illustration of whaling in the lagoons as the Frontispiece for his book *Marine Mammals of the North-West Coast of North America*. It was drawn years after his last whaling voyage and likely represents a composite of memories from sketches.

lined shores and distinctive flat-top mesas and hills to the east of the lagoon. He also drew maps of the lagoon's interior, which were some of the few reference materials we were able to find on the lagoon. While not a financial success, this volume received great acclaim from Scammon's academic and professional colleagues. Only a few original copies survive, and these are sought after by collectors today. His careful observations of the ways of the gray whales during their winter breeding and calving season in the Baja lagoons established the foundation for much of what we have come to learn about gray whales.

Nineteenth century whaling from ships and shore stations devastated the gray whale population taking it to near extinction. A market shift from whale oil to petroleum products and the early whalers' inability to pursue a species to its end probably saved the gray whale from complete extirpation.

A period of "modern commercial whaling" involving ships from the United States, Japan, Norway, and the former Soviet Union occurred from 1914 to 1946 and targeted gray whales and other species in the Pacific. During this period gray whales declined to critically low numbers, and finally received protection from the International Whaling Commission in 1946 under the International Convention for the Regulation of Whaling. That protection continues to this day. Native Russian Arctic communities are permitted a subsistence harvest of up to 140 gray whales each year. Two United States statutes provide further legal protection: the 1972 Marine Mammal Protection Act (MMPA), and the 1973 Endangered Species Act (ESA) prohibit the "taking" of marine mammals and the destruction of their habitats in U.S. waters.

In the absence of hunting pressure, the Eastern North Pacific gray whale population slowly recovered to an estimated 25,000 whales by 1990, and in 1994 the United States Department of the Interior removed it from the ESA's List of Endangered and Threatened Wildlife and Plants. In 1996 the World Conservation Union (IUCN) reclassified this population from "Endangered" to "lower risk: conservation dependent" on The IUCN Red List. The Western North Pacific gray whale population has never recovered and remains listed as "Critically Endangered" throughout its range. It was reclassified in 2000 from "Endangered" to "Critically Endangered" by IUCN.

Recognizing the importance of the gray whales' breeding lagoons, the government of Mexico established Laguna Ojo de Liebre (Scammon's Lagoon) as the world's first whale refuge in 1972. Then, in 1979 Laguna San Ignacio became a "Whale Refuge and Maritime Attraction Zone." Reserve status was extended to Laguna Manuela and Laguna Guerrero Negro in 1980. All of these bays and coastal lagoons lie within the larger El Vizcaíno Biosphere Reserve. Created in 1988, the reserve encompasses Laguna Ojo de Liebre to the north, Laguna San Ignacio to the south, the Sierra de San Francisco in the east, with the vast Vizcaíno desert at its center. In 1993, the United Nations Educational, Scientific, and Cultural Organization (UNESCO) made Ojo de Liebre and San Ignacio Lagoons World Heritage Sites. They are also designated Ramsar-protected wetlands under "The Convention on Wetlands of International Importance." Mexico continued to lead the way for protecting gray whales, and in 2002, all Mexican territorial seas and Economic Exclusion Zones were declared a refuge to protect large whales.

Today gray whales range from coastal Baja California and portions of the western mainland coast of Mexico, the west coast of the United States, to the waters of western and northwest Canada, Alaska, the eastern High Arctic, and east coasts of Russia, Japan, Korea, and the northeast coast of China where they receive varying degrees of protection, from absolute sanctuary to none at all.

2 First Impressions

Turn Left at "San Angle"

THE WHALERS OF OLD arrived by sea. Today there is a highway, and then a road leading to Laguna San Ignacio. The lagoon was located 50-kilometers across the desert from the town of San Ignacio. In 1977, the road was not much more than a dirt track that was generally bad or worse, depending on recent rains. A one-way trip to town could vary between four hours and all day, depending on the number of washouts and vehicle breakdowns. Once off the paved highway, we followed meandering rutted, rock strewn jeep trails across the desert. At a small rancho named San Angel we took a left turn in the road and began to cross a series of sand dunes that finally gave way to an expanse of open mud flats — the "Salitrales."

The road across the mud-flats, such that it was, consisted of two well worn tire ruts running across a mirage shrouded flat that extended to the horizon. If you stay in the ruts, you are OK. Should you stray off them, your wheels immediately become mired in slippery brown mud mixed with salt. Even when covered with standing water, the rule is "stay in the ruts." There is no vegeta-

The road to Laguna San Ignacio when dry.

tion for miles, but somewhere out there was the lagoon. Occasionally we came across a desiccated date palm tree trunk lying on the salt flats, washed down the canyons from the oasis by winter storms or "Chubascos." We were crossing the extensive flood plain that fans out from the San Ignacio river valley to the east. Flash floods wash trees down the valley and deposit them on the salt flats. Other sightings included the stripped, rusted shells of old trucks and cars permanently sunken into the mud. We dubbed these *Ferro carcass rustolia* and they come in many varieties.

After three days driving down the Baja peninsula, we received our first look at the lagoon we had tried to learn so much about in the preceding months. Our small caravan emerged from the mudflats to the north of the lagoon and intersected the road to the shore-side community known as "La Laguna." La Laguna is home to Sr. Francisco "Pachico" Mayoral and his immediate family. It was sundown and the sky to the west was crimson orange to the horizon where it met the indigo blue of the lagoon's water. It was calm but with sufficient chop on the

Driving across the the "Salitrales" after a rain.

Camping under a most spectacular umbrella of stars.

water to catch the orange from the sky in multitudes of sparkles against the deep blue green of the water. We saw no whales or whale blows in the dim twilight of the fast fading day. We heard the low cackling of hundreds of Brant geese as they settled in for the night on the exposed mudflats. Then the cry of an Osprey eagle as it winged off to its roost, a fresh caught fish swinging from its talons. And further in the distance the cries of coyotes beckoning the night's arrival.

After speaking with Pachico and his brother-in-law Chema about the roads along the shore, we set off again in the twilight to the location of our first camp. The spot was about four miles farther along the southern shore adjacent to another lagoon resident's home. One-hundred years ago "La Freidera" or literally the "fryers" was the site of the shore-based try works of whalers of old that harvested and processed gray whales there in Captain Scammon's time. Now Sr. Antonio Camacho and his family lived in buildings that stood on those early foundations, and fished the rich waters of the lagoon for a living. Sr. Antonio suggested that we park our van on the south side of his home to be out of the wind. We set camp by the light of our headlights along the eastern shore well inside the northern portion of the lagoon. For the first time we heard the sublime "whoosh" of whale blows far out in the lagoon in the dark. As we prepared and ate dinner we wondered what the daylight would bring. Under a sky filled with millions of stars, we drifted off to sleep to the sounds of those whale blows.

Fish Camps, Meros, Turtle, and Lobsters

"Good grief," we exclaimed. "It's an ocean!" These were our first thoughts at our first sight of the sight of the lagoon in the early morning sun. I guess we'd expected a smaller body of water. Dawn revealed water as far as we could see to the north and to the south. Laguna San Ignacio in 1977 was a near pristine inland sea surrounded by desert. We had selected Laguna San Ignacio for our study site because it was the current focus of U.S.-based whale watching tourism, and because it was only a third of the size of Ojo de Liebre (Scammon's) Lagoon to the north. It is approximately 160 km² and could be surveyed daily by small boat, weather permitting.

So began our exploration. It was mid-January. Already many whales were in the lagoon's interior. The museum had given us a small yellow inflatable boat and a 7.5 hp outboard motor. The "Metzler" was to be our vessel of exploration, and with it, we ventured out onto the lagoon for the first time. Not knowing exactly where we were, we set off to the north toward what appeared to be a large outcropping on the opposite shore. It seemed to be a huge uplifted portion of the desert floor, facing to the east, and forming a steep cliff face. It rose some 30 m above the shore of the lagoon while its backside gently sloped westward to the desert floor. After anchoring our boat we hiked around the side of the bluff and discovered numerous gypsum crystals on the ground and embedded in the rocks. Thus we named this place "Crystal Bluff" or "Cantil Cristal."

In the days and weeks that followed we circumnavigated the entire lagoon shoreline. In many locations we found the abandoned camps of the lagoon's fishermen. Some were no more than a woven palm frond sunshade on poles,

Ramon Grande and Ramon Pequeño unloading lobsters for the market.

A 1980s catch of very large "Mero" or Black Grouper.

while others included substantial plywood buildings for shelter from the winds. Scattered around the grounds of these camps were evidence of previous catches. Sea turtle shells a meter in diameter lay bleaching in the sun along with the gigantic heads of black groupers or "Meros." Their vertebrae had the diameters of tennis balls. Foot long lobster carapaces absent their tails were evidence of the gigantic crustaceans that roamed the depths of the lagoon. And 1–2 m tall piles of scallop shells were heaped along the shores.

We would learn later that these were seasonal fishing camps, occupied only during the months when certain species were the focus of the harvest, and that the principal target species would change over time in a cyclic manner. For example, lobster would be fished heavily for two or three seasons where upon they would become scarce. The emphasis would then switch to grouper and other fin-fish for a couple of years. And then shift to clams and scallops. By that time, the lobsters had recovered to marketable size, and the fishermen would again pursue them, and the rotational cycle would begin again.

At the time the local fishing pressure would not completely deplete one species group, but fish it down and then rotate to another that was more abundant. While this sort of rotation exploitation appeared sustainable, one fact was clear. The sun-bleached turtle shells, large grouper heads and bones were evidence of very old and large individuals that were no more to be found. The fishermen themselves were the first to admit that the "big ones" were fast becoming rare and that fishing pressure was increasing.

Punta Piedra

It was February of 1977 when we first landed on this rocky promontory jutting out into the lagoon. Our excursion that day had led us to the main channel of the lower lagoon near the entrance. The point was marked by a lone pole sticking 4-5 m in the air with two smaller boards nailed to it in the form of a cross. Sort of an "X" marks the spot, apparently a marker that aided fishermen returning from the lower lagoon and entrance with finding their way home in this region of low relief and few predominant landmarks. From time to time a young osprey would roost on this pole in the evenings. This fish eagle became sort of a camp fixture, and it didn't seem to mind our coming and going.

This was "Punta Piedra" or "Rocky Point," one of the local landmarks that Ray Gilmore had told us to look for. "It is in the center of everything" Ray told us, "A good place to camp, I suspect." Punta Piedra is located about one-third of the way into the lagoon from its ocean entrance. There, the main channel curves to the east and splits into three channels that meander northeast into the middle and upper lagoon basins. Here the ancient sandstone rock has been

First camp on Punta Piedra in 1977.

breached by eons of relentless tidal action that created a rocky channel about 1.5 kilometers wide from shore to shore. All of the water moving into and out of the lagoon moves through this constriction or bottleneck, which keeps it swept free of the sandy shoals that characterize the inner portions of the lagoon to the northeast, and deep water is near the shore at all phases of the tide.

From this point one has an unobstructed view down the lower entry channel to the surf and breakers to the west, and of the opposite shore. While sitting on its rocky shore we noted that, like the tidal flow, all the whales moving up and down the lagoon passed by Punta Piedra, and right next to shore. It was like standing on a busy street corner watching the passing traffic. Clearly, this was the place from which to base our observations of the whales. This site offered access to all points within the lagoon, and an unmatched observation perch in and of itself. But, the question was how to get there from our present camp at La Freidera well within the inner lagoon's southern shore?

Our maps, basic as they were, showed the area behind Punta Piedra as completely blank. The only features depicted along the lagoon's southern shore were mangroves and mudflats. Ray Gilmore had drawn in a large bay behind the point, but explained to us that he had only glimpsed it to the south from the nearby "Parmeter Island", or "Isla Abroa" (as it was locally known), and he had never explored it. We set out to find a land route from our mid-lagoon camp to Punta Piedra.

For hours we wandered around the desert behind mangrove estuaries that bordered the lagoon's southern shore hoping to find some route to the point. Very old tire tracks in the sand played out one by one and they either vanished or led to dead ends on the lagoon's shore. We finally negotiated a short stretch of mud flats that were exposed at the moment by the low tide, and crossed onto "dry" land again. We were hoping that we would find Punta Piedra somewhere to the west, as we drove down a very old and rutted road toward the shore. We saw two small shacks in the distance and upon arriving discovered the two abandoned fish camp shelters we had seen earlier from the water while exploring the lagoon interior. We later learned these were the seasonal fishing camps of Sr. Cruz Vicente and Ramon Ceceña from the town of Punta Abreojos.

From their fish camp, we could see Punta Piedra across a kilometer or more of water and mudflats. We could also see that thick mangroves surrounded the point. We continued searching along the mangrove's margin where they met the desert for a bridge to the point, but found none. Although connected to the desert by a series of mangroves and mudflats, the point was effectively an isolated island. We returned to our mid-lagoon camp knowing we needed to re-locate to Punta Piedra, but not knowing how we were to get there, or once there, how to go back and forth to the only road to the only town for 50 km?

Rocky Point Hilton

Two National Geographic photographers accompanied us on that first trip to Laguna San Ignacio. Ken Nelson and Bill Weaver stayed on Punta Piedra hoping to film friendly whales. They confirmed what we surmised: "Rocky Point" was the place to be in order to observe the daily activities of the whales and they dubbed their camp the "Rocky Point Hilton." Earlier the Geographic film crew had enlisted the assistance of Pachico Mayoral to guide them around the lagoon, and we now turned to him for advice. We explained our predicament in our broken Spanish. "No problem, I will move you to Punta Piedra" Pachico responded with a smile. The next morning he arrived and within an hour everything but our VW van was piled high in his panga. Once at the point, Pachico, Bill and Ken all pitched in to unload our gear. We spent the afternoon assembling an observation tower our friend Bob Mathers had fabricated from aluminum poles and braces. Just before sundown, with great pomp and ceremony we raised and placed it on the edge of the point. At a height of 5 m it was the tallest structure for miles, and afforded a vista in all directions. We dined on fresh clams, red wine, and flour tortillas made by Carmine Mayoral.

We settled in for the night along with a thousand deer mice led by "Mousey-Dung," another thousand lizards, a few dozen coyotes, and the sounds of whales blowing just a few yards outside our tent. The "Rocky Point Hilton" was open for business.

Our camp "Headquarters" on Rocky Point in 1979.

The Rocky Point "Hilton" research camp in 1980.

Watching Whales Go By

Mary Lou exclaimed "Altitude, we need some altitude," as we surveyed the expanse of very flat desert from the tip of Punta Piedra. Enter good friend and engineer Bob Mathers. Our charge to him was to produce a tower, five-meters tall, with little wind resistance, that could support two people, and that could fit inside a VW van. One day, Bob called and said, "Come look at what I've built." There rising out of his San Diego backyard was a five-meter tall viewing tower

Our observation tower on Punta Piedra.

Mike "Eagle Eye" Bursk and Mary Lou monitoring gray whale movements past Punta Piedra from the observation tower.

of aluminum tubing, that could be disassembled and transported in the back of our VW van. On top of the aluminum structure was a platform; a four-by-eight foot sheet of plywood enclosed by knee-high walls.

Once in place on Rocky Point, the observation tower was the tallest structure around and looked very much like an oil derrick anchored to the ground with guy lines. Once, while we were in it, a wayward frigate bird appeared to be on a collision course with the tower. Caught by surprise, he just wasn't expecting anything that tall out there in the desert! From there we watched the daily procession of whales move past Punta Piedra. It was our play-pen of sorts, and its short walls kept us from falling out in moments of exaltation when you think you've seen something really remarkable.

For the tower work, we developed a recording system to document and tally the number of whales moving into and out of the inner lagoon with the tides, and the paths they followed as they moved with and against the tides. Sitting in the tower for hours also allowed us to see behavior and interactions between whales that we would never have detected from a boat. It was apparent that the whales did not enter the lagoon to just sit there. It's a really dynamic system, with a steady two-way stream of whales flowing through the lagoon. At peak season we estimated as many as 500 whales a day may move into and out of the lagoon. In one seven-hour tower survey, while our previous survey count indicated there were 270 whales in the lagoon, at least 341 entered and 185 left. We reported this difference in the number of entering and leaving whales in one of our early progress reports. Little did I know that this would get the attention of two of the premiere cetacean experts of the day.

A year later while attending a marine mammal conference in La Paz, I was confronted by Drs. Kenneth S. Norris and William Schevell asking about this discrepancy in the number of whales moving into, but not out of the lagoon. Bill carefully explained that there had been a railroad company in New England that sent more trains north than ever returned, and the company later discovered that their employees were cutting the trains up for scrap and selling the steel. And so how could I explain the missing whales in Laguna San Ignacio? Realizing that they had me, I looked each of them in the eye and proposed that there might be underwater caverns that the whales used to travel under the Baja Peninsula into the Gulf of California to the east. "Go get 'em" bellowed Ken and we all had a good laugh. As fate would have it, years later Ken would become my academic advisor for my graduate studies at the University of California at Santa Cruz.

To get a better understanding of the dynamics of the whales' movement, we moved the tower around the lagoon. One season we positioned it off the north end of Isla Garzas in the northern portion of the lagoon, and another season we placed it on the northern tip of Isla Ana to monitor the entrance and exit of whales through the breakers at the mouth of the lagoon.

Eagle Eye

With confidence he said, "There it is again, over there to the left."

I said "I still don't see it. There is nothing there."

"Sure it is, right there to the left of the big dune on the shore, about 300 yards out and moving to the right. Watch the water," he said with conviction.

"Well, I still don't see what you are talking about. There is nothing there," I repeated. Moments later, a whale breached and in its wake surfaced a small calf. And so went countless exchanges with Michael K. Bursk, a.k.a. "Eagle-Eye."

We met Eagle during our first visit to the lagoon while he was working as a crew member on one of the whale watching boats out of San Diego. He had an interest in marine biology which he was studying in college, and he was very interested in what we were doing to learn more about the whales. His abilities as a fisherman, a boat handler, cook, photographer, navigator, and budding marine biologist made him an attractive addition to the project.

Best of all was his sense of humor. With inspiration from an ornithologist friend's habit of comparing all shore birds to a Willet, Mike invented new bird species like the "Hatchet" and the "Mallet" (a hand ax and wooden mallet adorned with colored feathers). He strategically re-located my prized plastic pink flamingos (a gift from friends) in a mangrove marsh and rolled with laughter when a visiting naturalist exclaimed to his tour group "My lord look at those! These are rarely seen down here!" He spent hours manufacturing fake arrowheads to leave on the trails for the lagoon visitors to find. He stomped out large dinosaur footprints in the sand leading out of the surf and into the mangroves, again for the delight of visiting natural history buffs. He could always find a fish for dinner, even at low tide. Mike is also a poet.

POEM FOR LOU

Distant thunder of offshore waves
Gulls scavenging
Low tide
Salty breeze rustling mangroves
Shorebirds feeding in our footprints
Our beach
Listening to captured seas roaring in the tun shell
While coyotes stalk us we stroll
Under gliding pelicans who pay little attention
To Sea Lions, who never notice us
Watching sunsets from a golden dune,
The wind arranges sand around our feet
You wonder what the winds of time will do
I don't know, but I'd like to find out

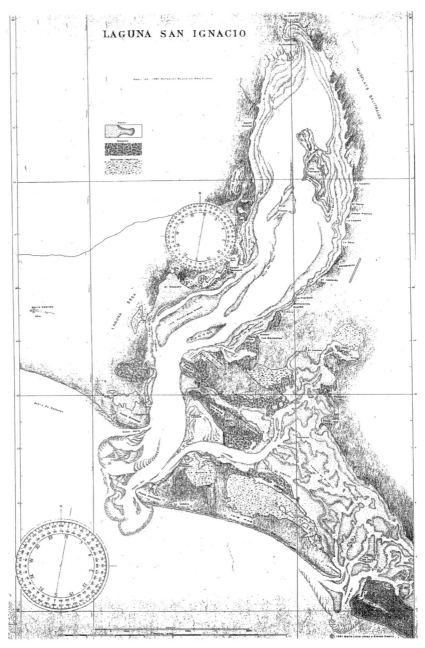

Our original map of Laguna San Ignacio used in 1980 showing deep water and shallow sand bars and mudflats. It compares well with a recent NASA satellite view (*opposite*).

Map Making

Ran aground again! The fishermen thought us odd as we set off across the lagoon on straight lines, only to hit obvious sand bars. Then carefully taking compass fixes on several prominent landmarks, only to push off and run aground again on the opposite side of the channel, all the while recording the channel depth with a battery operated depth sounder. Once we explained our behavior, it made good sense. By marking each landfall and the depth, we slowly but surely developed a reasonable chart of the lagoon's shoreline, interior channels and sand bars, complete with tidal differences.

The only previous charts available to us were drawn by Charles Scammon in the 1860s and published in 1874, and a 1907 United States Hydrographic chart. We had copies of each generously augmented with Ray Gilmore's notes and sketches. Compared with recent satellite photos, Scammon's chart was surprisingly accurate. At least the rocky points and hills had remained the same during the past century. The lagoon's residents and fishermen contributed the local names of the various locations around the interior, along with historical accounts of how those names were acquired. When completed in 1980, our chart was a big hit as there had never before been such a comprehensive document available.

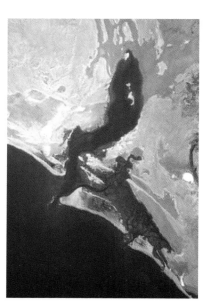

Features of Laguna San Ignacio

Crystal Bluff
North End
Isla Garzas
Isla Pelacino
Los Cerritos
Upper Lagoon
La Laguna
Middle Lagoon
La Freidera
Sand Hill
Punta Piedras
Bahia de Ballenas
Lower Lagoon
Estero De La Pitaya
North Entrance
Isla Ana
Gilmore's Lagoon
Punta Holcombe
South Entrance

0 1 2 3 4 5 6 7 8 9 10
kilometers

When It Rains It Rains

Laguna San Ignacio is usually bathed in subtropical sun and dried by relentless winds. When calm, the warm temperatures are chilled by offshore breezes and by cold Pacific water that rises from the depth and cools the shores of Baja California. These cool winds and warm desert frequently combine to create occasional fog. We were there during the winter, and "Chubascos" (winter storms of hurricane proportions) were occasionally endured. When the wind came up from the south we'd get nervous. It meant rain, and usually lots of it. We kept a reserve supply of garbage bags solely for bagging up everything that needed to be kept dry. The desert shore of the lagoon is flat, and covered with clay and shell soil, which when wet turns to mushy puddles of red mud. The worst was when it rained and the wind blew at the same time. This loosened the tent stakes and down the tents would come, usually at night, but not until the early morning hours just to add insult to injury.

One benefit of the rain was the awakening of dormant flowers and shrubs in the dessert. Before a rainfall, the desert was its usual dusty brown, with leaf-less, flower-less, life-less looking plants from horizon to horizon. Within days of substantial rain, the land would come alive with green plants, grasses, and flowers of yellows, white, blues, reds, and oranges. To the flowers came insects and humming birds by the thousands, all rushing to feed on the pollen and nectar of the short-lived flowering desert plants that soon faded until the next rain.

The morning after a torrential rain, the Sierra de Santa Clara were shrouded in clouds.

3 Learning About Gray Whales

T HE GRAY WHALE, *Eschrichtius robustus* (Lilljeborg 1861), is the only living species in the taxonomic family Eschrichtiidae. This "mysticete" or baleen whale family's morphology reflects a natural history adapted to seasonal migrations in relatively shallow continental shelf waters between subtropical breeding areas and cold temperate feeding grounds. Gray whales evolved a specialization for "suction-filter" feeding on benthic or bottom-dwelling organisms. However, gray whales also employ "skim" feeding methods as found in right whales (Balaenidae) and "gulping" techniques as used by rorqual whales (Balaenopteridae) to exploit alternative free swimming prey on the surface, near the bottom, and in the water column. The morphological adaptations accommodating this variety of feeding strategies caused academicians difficulty in determining where to place gray whales in the grand montage of cetacean taxonomy.

Gray whales have rows of baleen hanging from the roof of their mouths, used to filter small food items out of the mud and sand.

What's in a name — Gray, Grey, or Scrag?

Since its discovery, a variety of common and taxonomic names have been applied to marine creatures presumed to be gray whales. This has created confusion in the literature, some of which lingers still. Vague mentions about near coastal whales of the typical size of gray whales date as far back as the late ninth century from Norway. A mid-thirteenth century work from Iceland known as the *Speculum Regale* contains a list of twenty whale species, two of which may refer to gray whales, but inadequate details do not lead to confident identities. The work is believed to have included illustrations, but none have survived.

Two hundred fifty years later, English explorer and whaler Jonas Poole observed numerous whales around Spitzbergen. The following year he returned to the island under Thomas Edge with two ships for The Muscovy Trading Company of England to evaluate the possibilities for whaling. His orders on 31 March 1611 included a list of whales they might find there.

> *The fourth sort of whale is called Otta Scotta, and is of the same colour as the Trumpa having finnes in his mouth all white but not above halfe a yard long, being thicker than the Trumpa but not so long. He yeeldes the best oyle but not above 30 hogs' heads.*

Trumpa refers to the sperm whale. The entry noted this whale was smaller, with short, white baleen and an oil yield that fit a description of the gray whale more than any other species on the list. Other curious references exist from the mid-seventeenth century that suggest the presence of gray whales in the North Atlantic. Around 1640, Jon Gudmundsson described and created illustrations of a whale known to Icelanders as "sandlægja." F. C. Fraser translated the text:

> *Good eating. It has white baleen plates, which project from the upper jaw instead of teeth, as in all other baleen whales, . . . It is very tenacious of life and can come on land to lie as seal like to rest the whole day.*

Fifteen years later, another list of whales known to Icelanders was passed to Danish physician Olé Worm. He included a chapter on whales in his volume, *Museum Wormianum*, but here again, none of the twenty-two listed species can be confidently linked to the gray whale. However, there are presently forty-two species of cetaceans known in the North Atlantic, not including the gray whale. If one excludes the warm temperate and tropical dolphins and the five rare beaked whales that range south of Iceland, the list declines to twenty-one, including the small harbor porpoise. The gray whale must have been among the whales on the list, but it cannot be determined which one by name.

Jon Gudmundsson's illustration of a Sandlægja, presumed to be a North Atlantic gray whale. The modern Icelandic language still uses Sandlægja for the gray whale.

Additional seventeenth-century accounts from the North Atlantic and the shores of the Atlantic Seaboard describe what was most likely the gray whale, including one by David Pietersz De Vries in 1655 documenting Delaware Bay whaling from 1632 to 1644. Adriaen van der Donck of New Netherland, also in 1655, wrote a more detailed account about whaling off New York and in Delaware Bay. The size and season suggest a gray whale over other possibilities.

In his 1835 history of Nantucket Island, Obed Macy wrote that in the pre-1672 colony a whale of the kind called "scragg" entered the harbor and was taken by the settlers. This was perhaps as early as the mid-1640s. In 1725, Paul Dudley, then Attorney-General of the Province of Massachusetts Bay and a gentleman naturalist, wrote a letter describing the whales along the coast of New England. He provided a description of the "scrag" whale.

> *The Scrag whale is near a-kin to the Fin-back, but, instead of a Fin on his Back, the Ridge of the After-part of his Back is scragged with a half Dozen Knobs or Nuckles: he is nearest the right Whale in Figure and for Quantity of Oil; his Bone is white, but won't split.*

Johann Anderson described the "Srag-Whale" [sic] in 1746 in *Nachrichten van Grönland und der Straat Davis* (*Notes from Greenland and the Davis Strait*). He may have relied entirely on Dudley's description, but he did note two other common names —"Knotenfisch" (lump fish) and "Knobblefisch" (bump fish). From those he created the first Latin taxonomic name for the whale: *Baalaenam majorem edentulam dorfoverfus caudam nodofo*, which means: Large toothless whale knotty on back towards the tail. However, he lacked a conserved specimen and the name did not conform to the Linnaean structure.

In a move that would prove confusing later on, German veterinarian Johann Polycarp Erxleben described a whale in *Anfangsgründe der Naturlehre* and *Systema regni animalis* (1777), giving it the name: *Balaena gibbosa* from the Latin *gibbus* for "humped." He listed the New England scrag whale as the last of nine common names for the whale. However, in 1836, French zoologist Gorges Cuvier dismissed Dudley's scrag whale description as spurious. Later, John Gray questioned the validity of *gibbosa*, thinking the specimen was a previously described species of *Balaena*. Analysis more than a hundred years later suggested *Balaena gibbosa* may have been a compilation, including a humpback whale, although humpback baleen is black and Erxleben described the whale's baleen as white.

J. Hector St. John formulated a list of whales familiar in Nantucket in 1782, but did not include anything like the scrag whale. That whale had apparently become scarce due to Basque, Icelandic, Scandinavian, English, and New England whaling over the previous one hundred fifty years. It may have persisted into the 1800s because sometime before 1869, Captain Atwood of Provincetown wrote to Joel Asaph Allen (then compiling a catalog of whales off Massachusetts) mentioning that a scrag whale was occasionally taken there. But by that time, commercial whaling of all kinds had subsided considerably due to over fishing.

Meanwhile in the Pacific, Nantucket whalers working on English ships were the first whalers to encounter the gray whale in Baja California in 1795. They recognized the scrag whale they had known in Massachusetts. When the first Yankee ships arrived at Magdalena Bay in 1845, they too recognized the scrag whale. It seems that up until Charles Scammon began working the Baja California whaling grounds, this whale was known only as the scrag whale.

Removed from the workaday world of whalers, the taxonomy of this whale developed further in the 1860s. Sub-fossil remains from Gräsö, Sweden, were obtained by Swedish Zoologist Wilhelm Lilljeborg in 1861. He believed they represented a new form of fin whale in the family Balaenopteridae. He named the species *Balaenoptera robusta* from the Latin for "strong," highlighting the stout rostrum of this whale compared with the broader rostrum of the fin whale, *Balaenpotera physalus*. Lilljebord shared illustrations of the specimens with John Edward Gray at the British Museum. Gray questioned its assignment to *Balaenoptera*. He published his analysis in 1864, establishing a new sub-genus closely affiliated with *Megaptera* (humpback whale). Gray wrote:

> 3. *Megaptera ? robusta* — I have been induced to refer it to this genus on account of the high, triangular, roundish form of the canal of the spinal marrow of the cervical vertebrae, and the form of the lower jaw. Lilljeborg referred it to Balaenoptera on account of the form of the blade-bone; but the two species of Megaptera differ in the form of that bone. The rib, as well as the blade-bone, is more like that of Physalus than Megaptera, but I believe that it may be a genus distinct from both. These observations are founded on some drawings of the bones kindly sent to me by Professor Lilljeborg.

The two anatomists credited with the accepted taxonomic name for the gray whale: (*left*) Wilhelm Lilljeborg (1816–1908) and (*right*) John Edward Gray (1800-1875). Photos: Det Kongelige Bibliotek, Copenhagen, and the British Museum.

Meanwhile, Danish zoologists Daniel Frederick Eschricht and Johannes Theodor Reinhardt wrote about the scrag whale in *Om Nordvalen (About Northern Whales)* in 1861. A translation of that work appeared in *Recent Memoirs on the Cetacea by Professors Eschricht, Reinhardt and Lilljeborg*, edited by William Henry Flower in 1866. Though not having reviewed the specimens themselves, they commented on possible confusions between the scrag whale and other whales.

Scrag and Scrag-whale have been common appellations during at least 150 years, and, like the name of the right-whale itself, have at different times and in different places been applied to cetaceans quite different from one another.

They were referring to the whalers' colloquial names. The bowhead whale was known as the black right whale and Greenland right whale, but it is obviously different from the northern right whale. One apocryphal etymology of the name "right whale" suggests it was "the right one to kill," a notion that can be applied equally to both species. Herman Melville proclaimed in *Moby Dick* that the right whale was "the truest of all whales," meaning that it was the archetypical whale. The genus name, *Eubalaena,* means "true whale." Eschricht and Reinhardt suggested that scrag whale, like the right whale, was a common term used for several different whales with similar characteristics. However, when all known use of the term is taken into consideration and context, it may be that when the Nantucketers applied the term in coastal New England and again in Bahía Magdalena, they meant a very specific animal—the gray whale.

Daniel Eschricht was a Danish physiologist, anatomist, and zoologist known for his work in cetacean comparative anatomy. He salvaged beach-cast specimens to create one of the largest collections of cetaceans in the eighteenth century. His 1849 volume *Zoologisch-anatomisch-Physiologische Untersuchungen uber die nordischen Wallthiere*, established Eschricht as an expert on whales. Eschricht and John Gray were respectful colleagues on the leading edge of cetacean anatomy. In a strange coincidence around 1846, two specimens of an undescribed species of dolphin surfaced—one on the west coast of Denmark, and the other caught off Yarmouth, England. Almost simultaneously, Eschricht described the specimen as *Delphinus ibsenii* while Gray described his specimen as *Lagenhorhynchus albirostris*. Gray's description was published just ahead of Eschricht's, and so Gray's species name, *albirostris* for the white-beaked dolphin got priority.

As lagoon whalers were sending the gray whale to the brink of extinction, anatomists were figuring out the taxonomy of Lilljeborg's specimen on the other side of the world. Gray was developing his opinions about the genus when Eschricht died suddenly on a walk in Denmark in 1863. Gray honored his colleague by naming the subgenus *Eschrichtius*, but still allied it with *Megaptera*.

Daniel Frederick Eschricht
(1798-1863).

He raised it to full genus rank in 1865, and created the family Megapteridae for the two genera. (Gray was working only with bones, unaware that gray whales lacked the many ventral grooves of balaenopterids.) Lilljeborg accepted Gray's analysis for the Gräsö specimen that eventually became the holotype of the modern gray whale, but it would not be official for nearly one hundred years.

The American anatomist Edward Drinker Cope assigned several fossil specimens to *Eschrichtius robustus*, having discussed with John Gray how similar they were to *Megaptera*. About the same time, Cope had acquired a subfossil left jaw from a beach in New Jersey and a more complete skull from the Pacific whale fishery (Monterey Bay, California). From this collection he created a new genus *Agaphelus* for Exlerben's *gibbosa* in 1868 that included Dudley's scrag whale.

Cope was brash and not particularly careful, known for rushing an idea to print. He split the *Agaphelus* specimens into two species: *A. gibbosus* for the New Jersey specimen and Dudley's scrag whale, and *A. glaucus* for the Pacific gray whale. Here "gray" enters the nomenclature—*glaucus* means gray in Latin. Thinking about it further, Cope abandoned *Agaghelus* for the Pacific specimen in 1869, creating *Rhachianectes glaucus*, Latin for "gray rocky shores swimmer," a name perhaps influenced by Charles Scammon's impressions. This was the taxonomic name Scammon used throughout his publications.

At this time, three different genera and species applied to the same animal. Cope missed the opportunity to match Lilljeborg's subfossils with the California specimen. Gray recognized the similarities between the scrag whale specimen (*A. gibbosus*) and the gray whale (*R. glaucus*), placing them together in a new family, Agaphelidae. But he also didn't make the link to Lilljeborg's specimen and the genus he created, *Eschrichtius robustus*. English naturalist Richard Lydekker did make the connection in an encyclopedia article published in 1894.

Max C.W. Webber dismissed Agaphelidae in 1904 and created Rhachianectidae for the gray whale, *R. glaucus*. In 1937, A.B. Van Deinse and G.C.A. Junge set to comparing the subfossil material from the Atlantic with the features of the gray whale from the Pacific and concluded that Lilljeborg's Gräsö whale and the Pacific gray whale were the same species. This put *Eschrichtius* ahead of *Rhachianectes* as the proper genus. However, they chose *gibbosus* for the species name, indicating they thought *gibbosus* took priority over *robustus*. Thus, the subfossils from the extinct Atlantic population became the holotype for the living population of Pacific gray whales.

In 1951, John R. Ellerman and Terence C. S. Morrison-Scott at the British Museum put the family name Eschrichtiidae in place of Rhachianectidae, making it the only taxonomic family of cetacea named for an individual.

On closer analysis of Erxleben's 1777 description, Gerrit S. Miller, Jr. and Remmington Kellog at the Smithsonian argued that Erxleben's subject was not a gray whale. The name *gibbosa* lost support. By the time Dale Rice and Allen Wolman produced their extensive study of gray whales in 1971, *Eschrichtius robustus* had become widely accepted as the proper taxonomic name.

A General Description of the Gray Whale

With all of the lower-level taxonomic questions resolved, we are given the current generally accepted taxonomy of the modern gray whales:

Class: **Mammalia**
Order: **Cetacea**
Suborder: **Mysticeti**
Family: **Eschrichtiidae** (Gray, 1865)
Species: ***Eschrichtius robustus*** (Lilljeborg, 1861)

Gray whales are medium sized baleen whales that grow to 13–15 meters in length, and weigh 16,000 to 45,000 kg as adults. They are slow swimmers moving at an average of 6–7 km/hr, although they are capable of sprinting for limited distances. There is no significant physical difference between males and females, other than the distance from the genital slit to the anus being wider in males. Ages estimated from growth layers in the waxy earplugs in the auditory canal suggests males and females may live between 40–60 yrs, although one female killed in the 1960s was estimated to be 80 years old and pregnant.

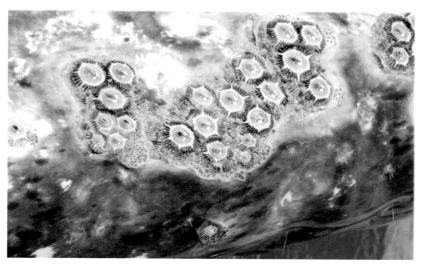

Barnacles and cyamid whale "lice" attach to the gray whale's skin, and vestiges of hairs protrude from shallow depressions along their head and chin.

The Body Form of the Gray Whale

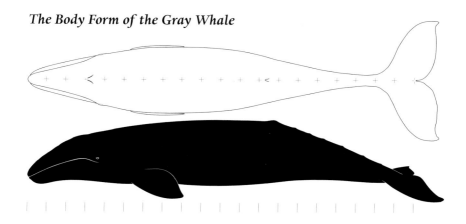

The Skeleton

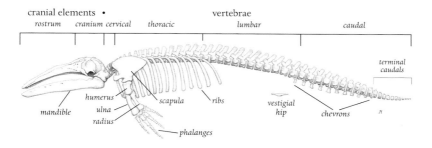

Their skin color is mottled light to dark grey with whitish blotches. They are hosts to a species-specific barnacle (*Cryptolepas rhachianecti*), and carry three species of cyamids or "whale lice"—*Cyamis scammoni* and *Cyamus kessleri* (that occur only on grays), and *Cyamus ceti* that also lives on other whales. "Whale lice" are not insects as the name suggests, but highly specialized crustaceans in the family Cyamidae, order Amphipoda. These symbiotic invertebrates feed on sloughing skin around barnacles, blowholes, in skin folds, and swarm into wounds. As such they may be beneficial to the whales.

The gray whale's head is elongate and triangular as viewed from above. The rostrum is moderately arched compared to the strongly arched rostrum of right whales and the relatively flat rostrum of fin whales. The skull is less telescoped than other mysticetes, and is relatively small at approximately 20% of their total length. They have a paired blowholes, or nares, located on the top and well back on the head, yet forward of the eyes. Coarse, cream to pale yellow colored

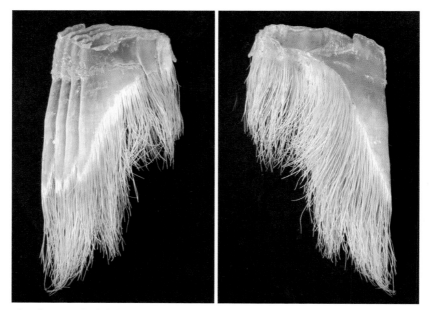

The photo on the left shows the anterior or front side of four baleen plates. The other photo is of the posterior or back side and shows how the frayed bristles of the inside form a sieve for expelling water and keeping the prey in the mouth.

baleen grows from the roof of the upper jaw. There can be 130–180 individual plates 5–40 cm long that are suspended from each side of the palate. Remnants of mammalian hair are represented by individual vibrissae that emerge from follicles on the rostrum and chin areas. Their throat typically has 2–7 short, deep, longitudinal creases that allow expansion of the gullet when feeding.

Instead of a dorsal fin, gray whales have a hump of variable size and shape, located on the back anterior to the base of the tail, which is followed by a series of fleshy knobs, or "knuckles," along the dorsal ridge of the tailstock. Their flippers are relatively short and paddle shaped, with rounded margins and pointed tips that become rounded from abrasion in older animals. The flukes of adults are broad, 3.0–3.6 m across and are frequently lifted before a deep dive. Unique to grays is a 10–25 cm wide "tailstock cyst" of unknown function on the ventral surface of the tail. The blow is 3–4 m high, heart-shaped, and bushy to columnar.

Known predators include killer whales and cookie cutter sharks. Gray whale remains have been found in the stomachs of some sharks, however, because sharks are scavengers of dead whale carcasses as well as predators, it is not known if ingestion of gray whale tissue was living or dead gray whales.

Gray whales possess a "double" blowhole on the top of their head (*left*), and grooves that allow expansion of the throat when feeding (*right*).

A dorsal hump and a series of bumps or "knuckles" adorn the back and dorsal ridge of the tail of gray whales. Left lateral view (*top*) and from the tail looking forward (*below*).

Gray whale flukes are "butterfly-shaped," dark gray in color, and accumulate many white scrapes and scars over time.

Like many other mammals, gray whales appear to exhibit a right or left dominance. As bottom feeders on the benthic mat, tube worms and other hard-bodied critters scrape against the side of the head that the whale presents to the prey mat. The barnacles and whale lice are rubbed off on that side. The whale in the photos above is right-dominant.

The distinctive columnar blow of the gray whale as viewed from the side.

Until recently it was believed that there were two recognized modern gray whale populations in the North Pacific: one in the Western North Pacific, which is depleted and critically endangered. It numbers a little over one hundred individuals and ranges along the eastern coast of Asia from Russia to China; and another in the Eastern North Pacific that numbers 21,000 or more and ranges along the west coast of North America. However, photographs of western gray whales obtained within the Baja California breeding lagoons of the Eastern population and on the feeding grounds along the eastern coast of the Kamchatka Peninsula demonstrate that both populations do mix to some degree. These photographs prove that some Western gray whales migrate with the Eastern gray whales to Baja California, Mexico in the winter where they may interbreed.

The fossil record tells us that the family Eschrichtiidae arose in the Mediterranean Basin during the early Pliocene about 3.6–5.3 million years ago. These early ancestral gray whales likely radiated across the Atlantic Ocean and into the Pacific Ocean through open Arctic passages or via the North Equatorial Current through the Central American Seaway that separated the North and South American continents prior to the emergence of the Isthmus of Panama. Siltation at the Isthmus filled in the Seaway about 4.5 million years ago.

The gray whale's eyes are positioned near the gape of the mouth and protrude slightly beyond the width of the skill and jawline. This orientation allows the whale to look forward and downward as it searches for food over the bottom. This may explain why curious whales will often approach a boat upside down to get a good look. With mouth open, a whale can look forward between the baleen and lip and see the tip of its snout.

If ancient Eschrichtiids did enter the Pacific Ocean via a Central American Seaway, they would have been archaic forms of the family and not the modern gray whale.

With the onset of Pliestocene glacial periods and falling sea levels, the Arctic passages between the Atlantic and Pacific became impassable due to the formation of persistent ice and a land bridge between Asia and North America, thus isolating the Atlantic and Pacific groups. All of the ancient forms went extinct, but the Pacific Eschrichtiids may have persisted longer than the Atlantic forms, hinting at the possibility that the modern gray whales emerged in the North Pacific. Evidence for this includes a Late Pliocene fossil from Japan aged at 2.4 million years old. The earliest "modern" gray whales are known from the Late Pleistocene based on a fossil dating 500,000 years ago from the Point Bay formation in San Diego, and a 220,000 year old skeleton from San Pedro, California.

Open water passages developed in the Arctic during subsequent Pleistocene interglacial periods, allowing gray whales to move from the North Pacific and re-occupy the North Atlantic. From these inter-ocean exchanges the modern gray whales left behind sub-fossil remains that date from more than 10,000 years ago and into the 1600s in the coastal regions of the North Atlantic, including Sweden, Belgium, the Netherlands, England, and from New Jersey to Florida in the United States.

Richard Cerutti, a SDNHM paleontologist, and his discovery of a
Pliocene Eschrichtiid skeleton in Chula Vista, San Diego County, CA.
Photo: Tom Demere, SDNHM

Gray whales, like many large cetaceans, are clearly long range explorers
capable of extensive migrations in search of suitable habitats and resources.
Support for these interglacial trans-Arctic movements was demonstrated in
2010 when a gray whale apparently migrated from the North Pacific across the
Arctic and into the North Atlantic, where its return to the Pacific was blocked
by the onset of winter and the icing up of the Arctic passage. This animal then
migrated south along the western European coast, and photographed in the
Mediterranean Sea off the coast of Israel! Then in 2013 another wandering gray
whale found its way to the coast of Namibia, Africa, the first historical record of
a gray whale south of the equator.

Weekly Whale Surveys

With the 1978 winter season we initiated a systematic effort to estimate the number of gray whales that were in the lagoon week by week from the beginning of the season in late-December until April when few whales remained. While the lagoon was 5–6 km at its widest parts, we soon learned that much of this was shallow water over mudflats that were exposed at low tides and not accessible to the whales even during high tides. The whales were confined to the deeper channels within the lagoon's center. Thus, from the whales' point of view, the lagoon was a long thin corridor averaging about 2 km across except for a large open basin in its northernmost interior.

We devised a plan to count the number of whales seen along a predetermined survey line that ran up the middle of the deep water paralleling the lagoon's axis from the entrance to the open basin at the northern end. Whales in the larger north basin were counted from a bluff on the northern tip of Isla Garzas which afforded sufficient altitude to see it all. While not a population estimate in the statistical sense, these counts (if obtained in a systematic manner) would provide an index of the minimum number of whales in the lagoon and trends in their abundance and distribution as the winter breeding season progressed.

Mary Lou and Steven prepare the Avon for a whale survey.

Steven and Mary Lou enjoying a night out aboard M/V Searcher when she visited the lagoon in February 1978.

We carefully laid out the course of the survey on our chart so as to split the areas of deep water equally on each side of the survey line. Two observers, one looking to the left and one looking to the right would count the whales as they passed the beam of the boat. The boat driver seated in the rear was responsible for noting whales directly on the survey line in front of the boat, and for making all efforts possible not to run over them. This became more and more of a challenge as the season progressed and whales crowded into the deeper channels near the entrance of the lagoon.

The first thing we discovered when we attempted to implement this procedure, was the lack of reliable landmarks available to denote turning points along our track. The place was so flat that although we could see from shore to shore along most of the survey line, it was difficult if not impossible to ensure that we would turn at the appropriate location to maintain our position in the middle of the channel. Except for a lone Cardón cactus on Isla Abroa, the tallest structure in the lagoon was our observation tower. We tried placing large square orange markers atop sand dunes at key locations, but these lasted only until the first good wind got a hold of them.

We finally developed a series of compass bearings to various prominent landmarks around the lagoon and the distant mountains. The start point at the entrance lined up with the great sand dune on the north shore and a saw-toothed mesa at the foot of the Sierra de Santa Clara to the north. The turning point that marked the transition from the lower lagoon to the middle channels was on a line between that sand dune and our camp on Punta Piedra. The middle lagoon channels transitioned into the middle basin on a line between the abandoned turtle camp on the north shore and La Freidera on the south shore. The channel to the upper basin began on a line between the northern edge of Los Cerritos (Double Hills) and the southern tip of Isla Pelícano. And finally, the upper northern basin began on a line between Cantil Cristal and the northernmost point of Isla Pelícano.

When plotted on graph paper these weekly counts illustrated the annual influx and duration of stay of gray whales into Laguna San Ignacio.

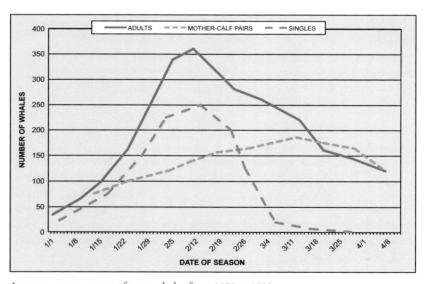

Average survey counts of gray whales from 1978 to 1982.

Gray Whales' Winter Timetable

Each autumn the Eastern North Pacific gray whales leave their summer feeding grounds in the Bering and Chukchi Seas and migrate southward 6,000 km or more along the Pacific coast of North America to the sheltered bays and lagoons of Baja California. Here the whales gather by the thousands to court and mate and to give birth to calves conceived the previous winter.

The southward winter migration of gray whales along Alta California is in full swing by late December, and by early January the whales begin to arrive at the Baja California lagoons in significant numbers. By early February the lower lagoon area nearest the entrance was full of mostly single whales, cavorting with each other for mating opportunities, and moving in and out of the lagoon with the tides. We observed females with newborn calves moving in and out of the lagoon, but they seemed to prefer the interior areas of the middle and upper lagoon basin. There, dozens of mothers and their calves moved about the channels and shallow water.

Judging from our weekly whale counts and the appearance of newborn calves, we determined that the greatest number of whales occupied the lagoon in mid-February, and about this time all of the calves of the year had been born. At peak season 300-450 adult whales and their calves could be counted inside the

lagoon with others outside in the surf and beyond the entrance, in the Bahía de Ballenas. After comparing the timetable of occupation for Laguna San Ignacio with other breeding lagoons, and the counts of migrating gray whales conducted off central California, it became clear that perhaps only a third (at minimum) of the entire population resides within the four Baja breeding lagoons at any one time during the winter. The remaining whales are spread out from the Gulf of California and the southern tip of Baja California Sur to southern California.

As the last of the fall's southern gray whale migrants reach Mexican waters, the first of the spring's northward migrants pass them on their return to their summer feeding grounds. Studies of whaling records by Dale Rice and Allen Wolman indicated that these first northbound migrants were the newly pregnant females heading to higher latitudes with its abundant invertebrate prey to feed and put on the blubber and body fat they would need to support their nursing calves the following year. The last to leave the breeding lagoons are females with calves of the year that have remained longer in the lagoons to give the calves time to grow and gain strength for the long northern migration.

Following the mid-February peak numbers, our weekly survey counts decreased and we saw few if any new calves. The distribution and dynamics of the whales also began to change. While counts of females with calves continued to increase week by week until mid-March. Counts of single whales (males and females without calves) steadily declined until, by March, virtually all the whales within the lagoon were mothers with calves. While the gray whales' annual birth period ends by mid-February each year, counts of females with calves continued to increase through March and into April as mothers with 2–3 month old calves continued to arrive at Laguna San Ignacio. Matches of our photographs with those from other researchers working in other gray whale aggregation areas confirmed that some of these whales were coming from Ojo de Liebre lagoon to the north, and Bahia Magdalena to the south. Why these mothers would bring their calves into Laguna San Ignacio before beginning their spring northward migration remains a mystery. We can speculate that it may have some social function allowing their calves to interact with other young whales, but we cannot be sure.

And with the departure of the single courting animals, females and their young abandoned the interior lagoon areas, shifted their distribution toward the entrance of the lagoon, and occupied the lower lagoon channel nearest the open ocean. Previously this was the domain of the courting single whales and the scene of their mating rituals. Now the females nursed and moved about the lower lagoon with their rapidly growing calves. Little by little, even their numbers declined until by late March and early April each year only a few pairs visited the lagoon's interior. Soon all of these whales would be well into their spring northward migration back to the productive feeding grounds in the higher latitudes of the Northwest Pacific coast of North America, the Bering and Chukchi Seas.

Recognizing Individuals

Photo-identification of individual whales was an integral aspect of our studies. Our friend Jim Darling had been photographing gray whales off Vancouver Island since the early 1970s, and he came to visit us that first winter in 1977. He had found, as had Mike Bigg with Killer Whales, that gray whales have distinctive permanent markings, such as variations in pigmentation, patterns, scars and scratches. Jim convinced us that, if photographed, these marks would provide information on the behavior and movements of each individual whale. We started photographing well marked whales. As each season passed, we came to identify individual whales by the distinctive colors and markings on their bodies. Eventually we assembled a catalog of photographs containing more than 500 different whales. Individuals that we recognized season after season were given nicknames such as Peanut, Rosebud, Cabrillo, Haleakala, and Pinto. Over the years this constantly expanding catalog proved invaluable in tracing the movements of those whales that returned each year, the duration of stay of individuals whales within Laguna San Ignacio, and movements of groups and individuals alike within and among the three major breeding lagoons.

The pigmentation pattern of the gray whale is a complex and random mix of mottled tonal values ranging from light gray to nearly black, with white splotches and spots, dark freckles, and lighter scars from barnacles and lice. Acquired scars from encounters with killer whales and fishing gear also provide unique markings useful in identifying individual whales.

By the spring of 1982 we had a large enough collection of photographs to compare them with other collections. Mary Lou met with our friends and colleagues Shirley Lawson, Susan Lafferty, and Peter Bryant, all from the University of California at Irvine, who had photographs of gray whales from Laguna Guerrero Negro and Bahía Magdalena, areas to the north and south of Laguna San Ignacio. Additional photographs from Laguna Ojo de Liebre (Scammon's Lagoon) were shared with us by Dave Withrow and his colleagues from the National Marine Mammal Laboratory in Seattle, Washington, and by a gray whale research team from Mexico's Secretaría de Pesca, or Ministry of Fisheries.

To our delight these collections contained a number of matching photographs that provided valuable new information about gray whales in Laguna San Ignacio and elsewhere. The first fact to emerge was that although some gray whale females return to the same lagoon each year, others circulated from one lagoon area to the next, and rearing their calves in different lagoons. Others visited different breeding lagoons in the same season. For example, one single whale photographed in Laguna Ojo de Liebre the first week in February and the following week in Laguna San Ignacio. Similarly, a female and her calf were photographed in mid-February in Laguna Guerrero Negro, and later in March in San Ignacio during the same winter. Another female was photographed in Laguna San Ignacio in 1978, in Laguna Ojo de Liebre in 1980, and then in Bahia Magdalena in 1982, each time with a newborn calf in a different lagoon.

By carefully noting which females had calves each year of our study, Mary Lou confirmed that most females give birth to a calf in alternate years, or 2.1 years on average. Other females may rest two or more years between calves, while one female produced two calves in two successive years, an exception to the general calving interval.

The number of days between when we first photograph a whale, and the last time we photograph it provided an estimate of the minimum length of stay for that individual in Laguna San Ignacio that year. Length of stay estimates allow another window into the behavior of the whales, and help to better understand the dynamics of the whales' use of this winter aggregation area. First we learned that single whales, "Solas" or breeding males and females without calves spend the least amount of time in the lagoon, averaging a week or less. Presumably these individuals, particularly males, move about within and among winter aggregation areas looking for opportunities to mate, and we re-sight them the least often.

In contrast to single whales, females with new calves spend the most amount of time in the lagoon with some spending a month or two with their calves in Laguna San Ignacio. These females prefer to rear their calves in surroundings in which they feel comfortable and not threatened. Laguna San Ignacio provides such a sanctuary, and the photographic re-sightings and numbers of female-calf pairs that utilize this lagoon during each winter bear witness to this preference.

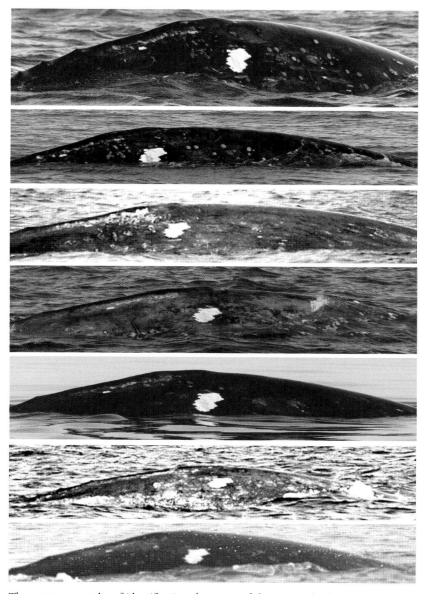

These seven examples of identification photos are of the same individual taken between 1996 and 2011. The images appear different depending on time of day, angle of light, lens used, position of the photographer, and other variables. However, key markings are sufficient to match these photos, giving researchers important data points on a variety of life history questions such as age, health, site tenacity, migration timing, associations with other whales.

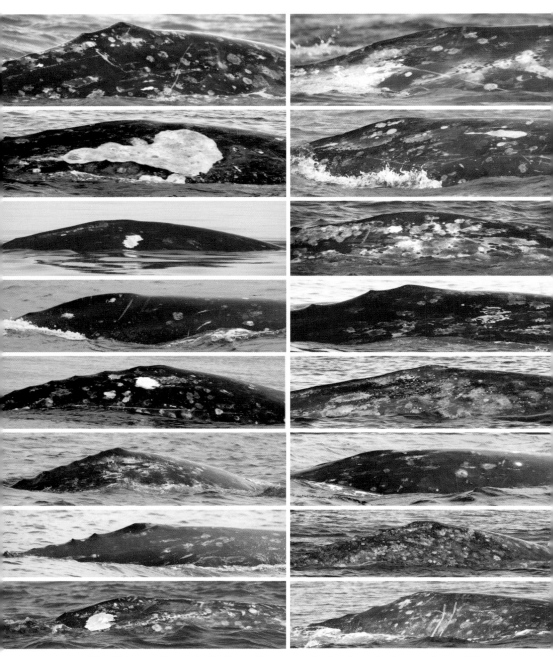

The distinctive "one of a kind" markings on the backs of whales form the basis of the photographic identification method for identifying individual whales. The photos on this page are of the right side of the whales.

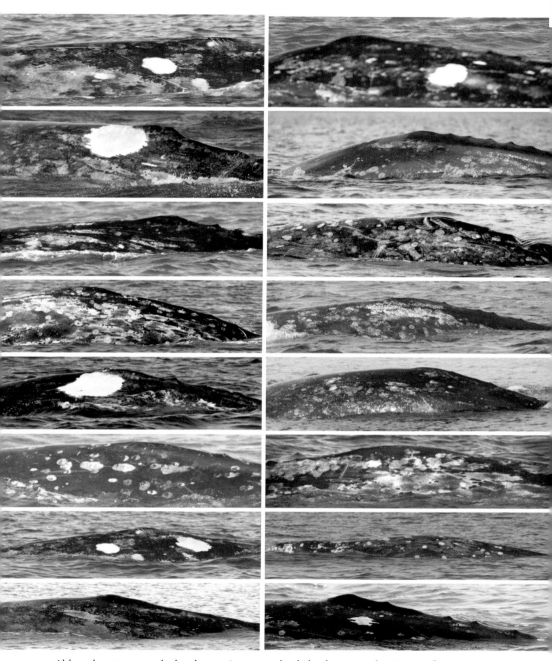

Although patterns on the head are unique to each whale, the seasonal variation of barnacles makes identifications based on head coloration difficult. The photos on this page are of the left side of the whales.

Courtship and Mothers and Calves

Our weekly surveys and analysis of photographs indicated that pregnant females carrying their near-term calves or those that have given birth during the
southward migration arrive in January, and following the birth of their calves,
may remain in the lagoons until April or even later. Mature females without
calves that are courting (what we called "singles"or "solas") also begin to arrive
in the lagoons in January and remain for periods ranging from a few days to a
few weeks to mate with the mature males.

Since gray whales normally calve every other year, theoretically only half
of the mature females are available for mating each season. Thus, logic would
suggest that mature breeding males outnumber females two to one, and this
fostered an early belief in the existence of a "ménage a trios" mating system
for gray whales, which was perpetuated by some naturalists. Gray whales are
mammals, and like all good mammals, this time of year male gray whales are
looking for opportunities to mate and pass on their genes. There are a number
of ways they can approach this.

One approach to a mating strategy would be to sequester a group of females and defend them and their territory from other males and mate with each
female as they became receptive, what behavioral scientists refer to as "poly-
gny." But this requires a lot of energy and time be spent on "defending" the

(*above and opposite*) Mating Gray Whales—the process begins with several whales close
together engaged in energetic swimming, diving, rolling, and touching.

dominant males territory and potential female mates. Another approach would be the "singles bar" strategy, where males spend their time and energy seeking out locations where females aggregate and try to mate with as many of them as they can even if they share them with other males. The females are concerned with conceiving a calf, no matter who the father may be. Our observations of breeding gray whales suggest the latter strategy is the norm. We learned that gray whale mating is a promiscuous, complex and uninhibited affair, with assortment of males and females mating with multiple partners.

Throughout January and into February we observed mating activities which sometimes blossomed into giant free-for-alls. These would involve as many as 18 to 20 individuals, complete with churning white water and flippers and flukes flying in all directions. As breeding animals heaved and rolled at the surface, quite impressive erect male organs, dubbed "Pink Floyds" by the whale watchers, revealed the aroused states of the participants. Then, suddenly the group would take off in a high speed chase, presumably with a female in the lead, which we

The gray whale "nursery" deep within the interior of the lagoon.

called "freight training." These chases could continue for a kilometer or two, only to stop again with the whales resuming their amorous courting behavior. Who actually sires a given female's offspring was therefore anybody's guess.

While all this breeding activity took place in and near the lagoon's entrance and in the deeper channels, gray whale mothers with recently born calves preferred to avoid the courting groups. They concentrate in the inner portion of the lagoon farthest from the busy entrance. This was their "nursery," the sheltered upper lagoon where the depth averages only three meters or less. Here, each February dozens of mothers congregate to rest or nurse their calves, and move with the tides. On calm days the blows of the females and their calves would hang in the morning air like down feathers caught in a breeze, and could be heard across the lagoon.

Some, but not all, calves are born within the lagoon, apparently a preferred and comfortable environment for the new mothers. As the eastern North Pacific gray whale population recovered, more and more females were giving birth during the southward migration, and we wondered how those calves fared compared to those born within the confines of a protected lagoon. Presumably, birthing and rearing their calves within the lagoon offers a survival advantage for the newborn. At birth gray whale calves measure 14 to 16 feet in length and weigh between 650 to 900 kg. They grow quickly on their mother's milk that contains 50% butter fat, one of the richest mammal milks ever reported. At winter's end and at the age of three months, it is time for the calves to leave the safety of the lagoon and begin their first northward migration. By then the calves have added three or four feet to their length and have more than doubled their birth weight.

As we watched mothers and calves in the nursery, it was apparent that growing calves have energy to burn, while their mothers, like mothers everywhere, are generally exhausted and appear to seek peace and quiet, and a nap when they can. In contrast, the calves were continuously active, nuzzling their mother's head and mouth, swimming onto their mom's rotund backs, only to slide off, roll across her massive tailstock, and pummel her with their leaping back-flops and belly-flops. Mothers appear very tolerant of all this and frequently join in, repeatedly lifting the calf out of the water, whereupon the calf rolls flailing itself back into the water with a splash. Calves also appear to frolic in Jacuzzi-like 'bubble bursts' that boil to the surface when their mothers release explosions of air underwater which boil to the surface.

A journal note from February 15, 1977 captured some of this:

"Yesterday Lou and I moved out to Rocky Point for a few days. We spent the early morning hours in agony on very hard ground, and a damp daybreak with fog. About 16:30 while observing whales from the tower we watched a mother and calf swimming into the falling tide just fast enough to remain in the same place - directly in front of us. While the female "treaded" water and held her position in the current, her calf surfaced repeatedly all around her blowing and making a general fuss. The mother several times blew bubbles while submerged and the calf would swim through these as they boiled at the surface. Twice the calf lurched onto the back of its mother as she surfaced, and stranded there only to roll off once more. Repeatedly the calf would "punch" its mother in the sides with it rostrum while continuing to swim all around her. Occasionally, the female would right herself and assume a prolonged "spyhop" or head-up position while the calf milled around her before resuming her upstream swim. What patience a gray whale mother must maintain with such an energetic youngster."

By late February females frequently gather in the lower lagoon and associate with other mother-calf pairs. Often groups of these whales will position themselves in the main channel of the lagoon, facing into the strong incoming or outgoing tidal current. The calves swim strenuously as if on a treadmill, going nowhere but getting a valuable workout which will prepare them for their first northward migration. For most, the migration will begin in March or April and last another three months before they reach the higher latitude feeding grounds. At some point during that first summer, calves eventually separate from their mothers as young whales.

Again from our journal dated March 15, 1978:

"In three months of observing these whales the calves have clearly undergone a transformation from relatively small, dark, rubbery, individuals with jerky movements to medium sized, well coordinated, miniature adults complete with mottled coloring. In three months they seem to have at least doubled in size, and perhaps grown even larger. The whales do not seem to regard the sun, tide, or wind. Their existence seems timeless. When we first erected our tower in January we could not count them all. Now in the final days of February two of us can easily keep track of most of their movements and activities. There are fewer whales in the Rocky Point area now, and I can't help but wonder how many of them have already left. Very soon many of them will go out to the breakers at the entrance of the lagoon and not return until next year."

A gray whale and her newborn calf move into the interior of Laguna San Ignacio.

With strength comes confidence, and the urge to explore comes to the grow-ing calves. Increasingly the calves leave their mothers for short periods to inves-tigate all manner of objects. We watched one little fellow entertain himself (or herself) with a ball of kelp, lifting the plaything onto its head, pushing it under-water, then releasing it to pop to the surface. When mother decided to move on, the calf followed obediently with the kelp securely perched atop its head.

While general wisdom suggests that only the toothed whales, like dolphins and killer whales, are social cetaceans, we were fortunate to spend sufficient time around lots of gray whales to begin to think otherwise. Within the lagoon we observed what we called "play groups" involving twenty or more pairs of females and calves, rolling and rubbing against one another, wheeling and div-ing and blowing blasts of bubbles. The calves run around chasing each other, "playing", and the females move around, splashing and lunging. At a distance all of this splashing and commotion would suggest that you were looking at a mating group of single adults. But when you start counting individuals, you'd find they were all females and they all had calves. We began to believe that this activity represents more than idle play. In the absence of aggressive courting adults, young whales meet their peers in these gatherings that appear to serve as opportunities for socializing. Here the calves begin to learn what it is to be a whale, and, perhaps even more important, to discover that there are other whales out there besides mom.

Their playful and coordinated activity suggested to us that gray whales must have a communication system, although it's unlikely they use echolocation or sophisticated dialects like killer whales, as no such sounds have been recorded around them. But they must use sounds for communication among themselves. For example, if a female wants to recall her calf from a group of calves, or if she's sleeping and decides to leave, she must utter some sort of signal, because the calf responds immediately and off they go. Except for extremely curious calves, who at times may become so engrossed with whale-watching boats and their passengers that their mothers must forcefully move them off when she decides it is time to go. So there's definitely communication going on between mothers and calves. Exactly how it's carried out and what its significance is under various circumstances, we do not know. The definitive work on the gray whale's song and vocal behavior is yet to be conducted.

Females are highly protective of their calves. During our third season we witnessed a striking example. From our observation tower on Punta Piedra next to a deep channel, we saw a calf thrashing as it left the channel and tried to cross over the shallow sandbar and stranded. Within a moment an adult whale we took to be the calf's mother surged out of the channel and beached itself beside the calf. Seconds later another whale beached itself on the other side of the calf, sandwiching the young animal between the two adults. Both adults then raised their heads and flukes, pivoted with the calf between them, and slid smoothly back into the channel. Quite surprised, we were not sure how to interpret what we saw, or that we would ever see such a thing again. However, the next year we saw it happen again at the same location in front of Punta Piedra. In each case the entire incident lasted only fifteen or twenty seconds and appeared to be a deliberate, well-coordinated act. Presumably one of the adults was the calf's mother, but the relationship of the other adult whale remains unknown.

A gray whale calf rolling off its mom's back.

Ups and Downs of the Population

During our study from 1977 to 1982 the United States National Marine Fisheries Service estimated the size of the Eastern North Pacific population of gray whales at between 19,000 and 21,000 individuals and increasing at 3–4% each year. By 1987 the population reached its maximum size at around 26,000, and in 1994 the eastern North Pacific gray whale was removed from the Endangered Species List. Then something unexpected happened: beginning in 1998 gray whales began to strand in unusually large numbers throughout their entire range from Alaska to Mexico. This mortality event affected all age classes of whales from yearlings to adults of both sexes and resulted in a ten-fold increase in the average annual stranding rate during the three year period from 1998 to 2000. The stranded whales appeared to be skinny and suffering from nutritional stress. A follow-up census in 2000 suggested that the population had been reduced by 20% to 16,000 individuals.

Years later we would learn that a decade long oceanographic regime shift during the 1990s in the North Pacific associated with the loss of permanent sea ice in the Arctic had disrupted the food chain that the gray whales and other species depended upon for food during the summer months. Simply put, the gray whales were not finding enough food to make it through the following win-

Photographs confirmed that in March some females with 1–2 month old calves move into Laguna San Ignacio from other areas.

ters. This was particularly hard on pregnant females that had to feed sufficiently during the summer to restore their own body fat, and to put energy into their developing calves. Following the mortality event our photos of gray whales in Laguna San Ignacio from 2006 to 2009 indicated that 10–12% of the individuals were showing some signs of nutritional stress, and looked skinny or "flaca."

As the years progressed, fewer and fewer photographs from Laguna San Ignacio included skinny whales, suggesting that gray whales were re-establishing their summer feeding patterns, and finding sufficient food during the Arctic summer. The NOAA Fisheries scientists also documented increasing numbers of gray whales in their official census of the population in 2007, a sign that the gray whale population was recovering from the mortality event of 1998–2000.

It was during the period from 2006 to 2010 that we saw the lowest numbers of new calves ever recorded in Laguna San Ignacio, suggesting that either there were fewer breeding females following the mortality event, fewer whales were selecting Laguna San Ignacio as a place to rear their calves, or that females once pregnant were having difficulty carrying their calves to full term and birth. Estimates of the calving interval (the number of years needed to produce a calf) based on photographs of known females supported the latter interpretation. Before the mortality event, Mary Lou had calculated a calving interval of 2.10 years based on records of 24 breeding females photographed with or without calves over a six-year period from 1977 to 1982. Estimates of calving interval based on photographic records of females during the 1990s and during the mortality event showed that the interval had increased to 2.25 years. Jessica Robles, a graduate student from the Autonomous University of Baja California Sur, analyzed a third set of photos taken from 2005 to 2011 and found the calving interval had further increased to 2.33 years during this period, which suggested that breeding females were producing calves every three to four years rather than in alternate years.

It was with relief that beginning in 2011 we witnessed a return of the late season pattern of occupation of Laguna San Ignacio by female whales and their calves similar to that seen during the late 1970s and early 1980s. Once again females and their calves were entering Laguna San Ignacio late in the season, and judging from the size of the calves, these whales were 2–3 months old and arriving at Laguna San Ignacio from other areas. Their numbers continued to increase well into April, and photographs confirmed that some of these whales were coming to Laguna San Ignacio from Bahía Magdalena in the south. We had not seen this pattern since the 1980s, and we were pleased to see the return of the late season females and their calves. And it was especially good to see that these calves and their mother were looking very plump and healthy once again.

Over the years we've found the photographic-identification methodology provides a rich source of information for monitoring the behavior and health of the gray whales. Despite environmental challenges that they encounter, the gray whale appears to remain "robust" in its ability to cope with and adapt to changes.

Beyond the Lagoons

Gray whales, like many large cetaceans, are clearly long range explorers capable of extensive migrations in search of suitable habitats and resources. Support for these inter-glacial trans-Arctic movements was demonstrated when a gray whale appeared surprisingly in the eastern Mediterranean Sea off of the coast of Israel. It had apparently migrated from the North Pacific into the Arctic Ocean to forage along the north coast of Canada, which is common and normal for gray whales. Presumably, this whale (and perhaps others) worked so far east that its return to the Pacific was blocked by the onset of autumn and the rapid icing up of the Arctic passage. With its return route blocked, this animal migrated south along the western European coast, and, in May 2010, researchers from the Israel Marine Mammal Research and Assistance Center (IMMRAC) photographed it a mile and a half off Herzliya Marina, just north of Tel Aviv, and then again along the Spanish coast in the Mediterranean Sea.

There is no doubt this is a gray whale in the Mediterranian Sea. It is the first known occurrence of the species in that part of the world. Photos: Aviad Scheinin, IMMRAC.

Then in May of 2013 another wandering gray whale—a whale obviously different than the whale in 2010 in the Mediterranean, was photographed in Walvis Bay, Namibia, by researchers from the Namibian Dolphin Project. This sighting off the African coast represents the first record of a gray whale ever south of the equator.

The Namibian gray whale appeared to be nutritionally stressed as suggested by the depression at the "neck" in the photo above, but this could be considered normal considering the time of the year. Photos: The Namibian Dolphin Project.

The best guess as to what facilitated the surprise appearance of gray whales in the Atlantic for the first time in more than two hundred years was an anomalously low Arctic summer sea ice extent in 2007 and again in 2012. This was due in part to the warming trend of the previous two decades and a strong Arctic cyclone in early August 2007 that sat over the North Pole for several days, chopping up the peripheral ice. Satellite images show when it was physically possible for gray whales foraging in the eastern Canadian Arctic to make the passage, and why a month later the route was blocked again by early autumn sea ice.

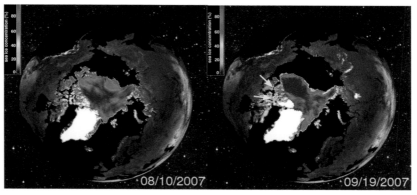

The Northwest Passage completely opens following a cyclone (*left*) and closes in two areas a month later (*right*). Images: University of Illinois, Dept. of Atmospheric Sciences.

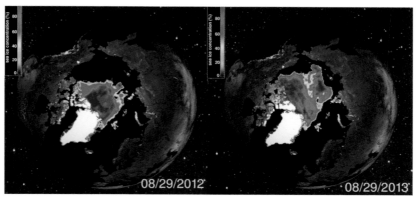

The Northwest and Northeast Passages open in the summer of 2012 (*left*), but the Northwest Passage did not open at all in 2013 (*right*). Images: University of Illinois, Dept. of Atmospheric Sciences.

4 Biogeography of Laguna San Ignacio

Early Physical History of the Lagoon

L AGUNA SAN IGNACIO is located on the Pacific coast of Baja California adjacent to Bahia Ballenas, approximately 680 km south of the international border between the United States and Mexico. The lagoon is part of the Vizcaíno Desert and borders a gently sloping, dry, coastal flood plain with sediment material dating to the late Cretaceous period and Paleocene epoch. Over millions of years of geologic uplifting followed by erosion, rivers washing rocks and sand from the mountains covered the region with alluvium of polished boulders, rocks, pebbles, and limestone deposits. The Pleistocene (beginning 2.5 million years ago) was characterized by multiple episodes of global cooling and the formation of glaciers over much of North America. These cold episodes resulted in repeated lowering of sea level and accelerated erosion on the exposed continental shelf areas.

A dust storm over Baja California in November of 2011 continued the ancient process of sculpting the landscape. Nutrients blown from land help fertilize the oceanic waters, promoting major phytoplankton blooms that attract many varieties of whales that feed in the region. Photo: NASA/Goddard, MODIS (Moderate Resolution Imaging Spectro-radiometer) on the Aqua satellite.

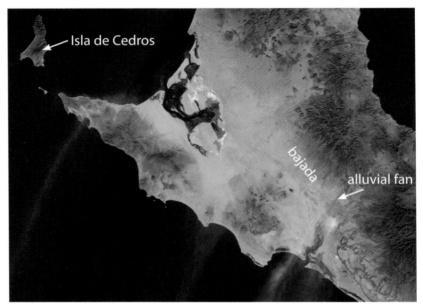

A view of the region from space showing the present-day lagoons and evidence of ancient shorelines. Photo: NASA/Goddard, MODIS on the Aqua satellite.

Alternating with the Pleistocene glacial periods were warm periods called Interglacials during which the sea level rose. The resulting coastal wave action further eroded the coastline of North America, forming marine terraces which are visible on the islands and much of the Baja California coastline today.

During the Eemian Interglacial approximately 135,000 to 105,000 years ago, the average global sea level was several meters higher than present for thousands of years. Shallow seas covered much of Baja California. Today's elevated marine terraces with layers of marine sandstones bearing marine shells and fossils are evidence of this period. Several ancient shorelines can be seen in photographs taken from space. On the ground, prominent ridges of sandstone and shell conglomerate bear witness to the ancient shallow seas that created them.

Evidence that Punta Piedra and Isla Abroa are former ancient barrier islands is found in their sandstone rocks, which are locally referred to as "chochina." These are filled with diverse accumulations of fossil shells cemented in the Pleistocene marine sandstones.

At the most extreme of the last Pleistocene glacial period, sea levels dropped as much as 120 m below its current level, exposing much of the continental shelf along the west coast and connecting some of the present-day islands to the mainland. Around 15,000 years ago, sea levels began to rise as the great northern ice sheets melted. Work by archaeologists from California State University Northridge for the Proyecto Arqueologico Isla de Cedros have shown that Cedros was connected to the Baja California peninsula with early inhabitants settling in several localities on what is now an island, dating to the earliest times of human habitation in the American southwest 9,000 to more than 10,000 years ago. As the seas rose, Isla de Cedros became isolated from the mainland around 7,500 years ago. Between about 6,000 years ago and today, sea levels have fluctuated as much as 3 m higher to lows of 1.5 m below present-day levels, further eroding the shore and near-shore archaeological evidence.

The area endured significant climate swings during this modern Interglacial, from subtropical forests to severe deserts. Extreme pluvial weather events filled valleys between mountains with sediments as ancient rivers transported rocks and sand into the coastal basins, transforming shallow bays into estuaries and eventually flood plains. The results of this process can be seen from high above, including the alluvial fans (sediments left by rivers or floods) and bajada (coalescing alluvial fans and outwash slopes creating wide deposits at the base of mountain ranges, from the Spanish "to go down").

The region's climate is now arid with an annual average rainfall of about 10 cm which falls mainly during winter months. This is supplemented by frequent coastal fog and heavy dew-fall along the coastal region. Temperatures range

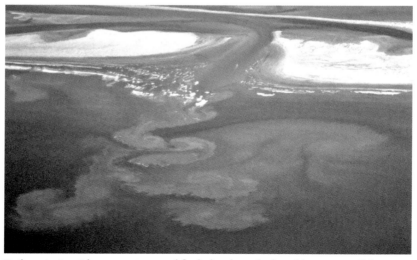

Daily outgoing tides concentrate and flush the phytoplankton blooms out of the lagoon's channels.

The lower lagoon from Rocky Point (Punta Piedra) at high tide and at low tide (*opposite*).

from 10°C to 25°C in winter. Freshwater streams or rivers no longer flow into the lagoon and miniscule runoff from seasonal rains has no effect. Laguna San Ignacio owes its existence to the twice daily tides that may run up to 3 kts during the full and new moons, and prevent sediments and sand from silting in the lagoon's channels over time. Many of the lagoon's deepest channels have well swept rocky bottoms, which are home to lobster, green turtles, and varieties of fish. The influence of these tides diminishes with distance from the inlet or mouth of the lagoon. Each outgoing tide flushes Laguna San Ignacio of its contents, and the incoming tide brings cold, nutrient rich sea water into the lagoon from offshore. As this water warms under the desert sun, the phytoplankton begins to bloom and within hours the waters turn green with microscopic plants. These are food for a myriad of shellfish and other filter-feeding invertebrates, and along with eel grass and other algae, they form the basis of the lagoon's marine food chain.

Laguna San Ignacio is basically a system of narrow, relatively deep channels surrounded by large intertidal sand and mud flats. It lies on a north-to-south axis, extends inland approximately 32 km, ranges from 2 km to 6 km wide, and has a area of 160 km², of which only approximately 60% or 90 km² is of sufficient depth (> 2 m) to be navigable by whales. The area of the inlet is approximately 20 km², and the east channel adds approximately 4 km². The semidiurnal tide ranges from 1 to 2.5 m, and the tidal currents in the inlet and channels can be very turbulent during extreme tides.

This lagoon has a distinctive topography characteristic of lagoons with an appreciable tidal range. The lagoon interior may be divided into five areas: the Inlet, East Channel, and the Lower, Middle and Upper Lagoons. The 4 km wide

Inlet is defined by a line of surf and breakers and includes a 1 km wide entry channel with a depth of up to 20 m at its southern end. The inner "delta" comprises many narrow channels running through sand bars and shallows with an average depth of 4 m. A steep walled Inlet channel runs northward inside the lagoon, parallel to the west shore of a large barrier island known as Isla Ana. The "delta" ends approximately 2 km inside the Inlet where the channel widens and deepens over its entire width. Here begins the Lower Lagoon which contin-

Some of the expansive mud flats of Laguna San Ignacio exposed at low tide.

Sierra Santa Clara and Morro Amarillo viewed from the entrance to Laguna San Ignacio.

ues northward to Punta Piedra, a rocky outcropping on the southern shore that forms a 2 km wide constriction in the lagoon.

The Lower lagoon is a relatively steep walled channel over its entire length with maximum depths of 25 m, averaging 3 km wide, with many irregular rocky and sand ridges running perpendicular to the lagoon's axis. The bottom in the area just south of Punta Piedra is characterized by 4–6 m tall rock outcroppings and valleys with sandy bottoms. To the northwest across the lagoon from Punta Peidra is a large sand dune that rises out 50 m above the desert. This is "Morro Amarillo" and is a prominent landmark that was noted on whalers' charts from the 1850s. The Lower Lagoon area was designated by the Biosphere Reserve as the "whale-watching zone" in the management plan for Eco-Tourism in Laguna San Ignacio. The remaining two thirds of the lagoon north of Punta Piedra is closed to whale-watching boat traffic during the winter as a sanctuary for breeding gray whales and their calves.

North of Punta Piedra begins the Middle Lagoon, a system of three channels separated by large shallow sand flats, and ranging from 7.6 m to 21.3 m deep. These merge into a shallow basin opposite of La Freidera, the site of the whalers' camp in the 1850s and now a ranch that hosts whale-watchers. The northern-most channel of the Middle Lagoon has silted in since we first surveyed it in the 1980's, and is no longer passable at its eastern end.

The Upper Lagoon begins at La Freidera and is a gently sloping basin averaging 5 m deep in its middle and 2 m or less at its northern-most end. Prominent land marks along the northern shore include "Los Cerritos" or Double Hill, and "Cantil Cristal" or Cristal Bluff named for its deposits of gypsum crystals.

The Upper Lagoon contains two islands, Isla Grazas and Isla Pelicano, which are connected by a shallow isthmus which is exposed at low tides. When we first surveyed these islands in the 1980s they hosted literally thousands of ground nesting marine birds (pelicans, cormorants, egrets, terns, gulls, etc.) and North America's densest aggregation of ground nesting Osprey. Unfortunately, over the years coyotes made their way onto the islands and destroyed the bird colonies. No longer a safe nesting or nighttime roosting location, the bird popula populations that once populated these islands have moved elsewhere and are now only a shadow of their former grandeur.

The areas at the head of the lagoon north and east of the islands are very shallow, with fine sand, silt and clay bottoms. The shoreline to the east slopes gradually into desert salt flats or mud flats which frequently flood with ocean water during high tides. Here at several locations sea water repeatedly trapped over the years has evaporated and created natural deposits of white salt, often several meters thick. The lagoon bottom in this shallow area once supported dense stands of eel grass that provided food for marine turtles, and contained a variety of crustaceans, gastropods, pelecypods, encrusting hydroids, sponges, and tunicates. Over the years gradual warming of the water in this shallow basin allowed the proliferation of brown-filamentous algae which has replaced the eel grass meadows.

Mountain ranges surround the lagoon on three sides, with their western slopes gradually declining into the coastal desert which eventually reaches the Pacific Ocean. To the east of Laguna San Ignacio is the Sierra de San Francisco, lying just below mid-peninsula it is the northernmost of the many volcanic

The freshwater oasis at the town of San Ignacio, 60 km east of Laguna San Ignacio.

peaks in Baja California that reach elevations of 1,600 m. These mountains are the source of the subterranean aquifer that surfaces in the town of San Ignacio 50 km east of the lagoon. There it forms a spectacular fresh water lake surrounded by lush stands of reeds and rushes characteristic of a freshwater oasis. The entire valley is filled with thousands of date palms planted by the missionaries when the settlement was founded.

This lake is the origin of the San Ignacio river which flows westward from the town approximately 30 km before it subsides underground. Along the river's route the ranches of San Joaquin, San Zacarias, and El Alamo are located where the water comes to the surface forming a series of "mini-oasises" at which a variety of crops have been cultivated by many generations of local families.

To the southeast are Las Tres Vírgenes, three spectacular volcanic peaks that top 2,000 m and can be seen from throughout the peninsula. They are believed to have been active as recently as the Mission period in Baja California in the 1600s through the 1700s. They are also presumably the source of volcanic glass or black "obsidian' which was used by the native populations to fashion arrow and spear points, and frequently found in the numerous shell middens and ancient camp sites around Laguna San Ignacio.

To the north of the lagoon are the Sierra Santa Clara, comprised of several spectacular spires jutting into the desert sky. These are the remnants of an ancient volcano cores or lava plugs suggestive of those found in Monument Valley in New Mexico in the United States. This series of vertical peaks lie between Laguna San Ignacio and the larger Laguna Ojo de Liebre to the north. The open desert around these peaks constitute the current range of the endangered Pronghorned antelope, or Berrendo (*Antilocapra americana peninsularis*), a subspecies of the North American antelope endemic to Baja California. In the 1980's these animals were restricted to the desert south of Laguna Ojo de Liebre and north of the Santa Clara's. In recent years we've found fresh foot-prints of these antelope in the salt flats and tidal areas along the northern shores of the Laguna San Ignacio. This suggests that conservation efforts for these animals are resulting in the recovery of their population and an expansion of their range within the Biosphere Reserve.

"Berenndo" (*Antilocapra americana peninsularis*), an endangered subspecies of the North American Antelope that resides within the Vizcaíno desert of Baja California.

Mangroves — Where the Desert Meets the Sea

As a child, my parents took us to Disney Land where I fell in love with the Jungle Boat Ride. Artificial as it was, around every turn in the river lurked something surprising—a group of gorillas on the shore, a hippopotamus surfacing to charge the boat, or having the boat almost crash into a waterfall. The extensive mangrove estuaries that ring the shores of Laguna San Ignacio brought this fantasy ride into reality, with an adventure of one kind or another around every corner.

Exploring a mangrove estuary was always a welcome diversion, especially on windy days when we had a high tide that allowed us to take our boat deep into the back channels. As these channels wind their way back into the desert, they split and become progressively smaller and smaller. We discovered that we were not the only creatures looking for sanctuary from the driving winds. Around each corner every branch seemed to hold birds seeking shelter from the wind. There were Yellow-crowned Night-herons (*Nycticorax violaceus*) announcing their presence with a loud squawk as they leaped into the air, only to glide off over the mangroves to find a new more secluded perch in the thicket. Reddish

Where the desert meets the sea—a rich habitat for marine life and birds.

Red mangroves are preferred nesting and shelter for many marine birds.

egrets (*Egretta rufescens*), Snowy Egrets (*Egretta thula*), Great Egrets (*Ardea alba*), White Ibis (*Eudocimus albus*), and mangrove warblers (*Dendroica* sp.) were abundant. In the channel's waters shoals of Corvina (*Cynoscion* sp.) swam among the mangrove's prop roots. Little Green Herons (*Butorides virescens*) stalked smaller prey in the lower branches. We could see clusters of small brown oysters and barnacles encrusting the exposed prop roots of red mangroves.

An abundance of salt tolerant plants and shrubs ring the perimeter of the "mangroves."

We followed the channel to its end where lagoon's water met dry desert sand. Within a few yards a diverse and biologically rich marine environment transitioned into an arid sandy, sage brush studded landscape. Only a thin band of cord-grass (*Spartina* sp.) and pickle weed (*Salicornia* sp.) separated these two worlds. Groups of Greater Yellowlegs (*Tringa melanoleuca*), Willets (*Catoptrophorus semipalmatus*), and Marbled Godwits (*Limosa fedoa*) were hunkered down in the grass for shelter.

It is here that one of the most interesting aspects of Laguna San Ignacio may be found along these interior shores. With each rising tide the Pacific's water surges inland to meet the arid desert, and a fascinating transformation happens. The apparent sparse desert scrub and sand suddenly burst into prolific and extensive saltmarshes and mangrove estuaries composed of diverse communities of green plants and provide specialized habitats for multitudes of marine organisms and birds. All of these plants are "halophytes," plants especially adapted to exist in salty sea water. In fact they thrive there because they have developed ways to survive the hypersaline conditions created by the flooding tides. Some concentrate salt in portions of their tissues, and periodically these drop off of the plant. Others actively excrete salt from their leaves. As a result, these envi-

White Mangrove thrives on the outer margins of the marshes where their extensive "air-roots" spread out under the sand.

ronments are one of the world's most productive sources of organic material that then supports other forms of marine life.

At the margins where sea water intrudes into the sandy desert soils you begin to notice reddish and black films of organic material covering the sand and rocks. These are diatoms and bacteria, some of the simplest and most primitive of plants and organisms, unicellular but each individual linking to others and forming films and mats of material that cover the substrate. Small marsh snails by the millions thrive on the diatoms and algae that are exposed with the falling tides in these margin areas. Some Cyanophyte bacteria, one very ancient of the earth's life forms, extrude filaments and excrete carbonates that bind sand grains into lumpy structures that may cover relatively large areas on sandy shores. These simple structures are one of the first phases of sand bar development that ultimately leads to lagoon formation. As you move further down the tide line we begin to encounter bands of low succulent vegetation lining the sides of tidal channels that are dominated by Salt Cedar (*Monanthochloe littoralis*), Pickleweed (*Salicornia pacifica*), Iodine Bush (*Allenrolfea occidentalis*), and Cordgrass (*Spartine foliosa*). Moving toward the lower shoreline we find margins of Cordgrass, Saltwort (*Batus maritina*), and Glasswort (*Salicornia bigelovii*). The

The Red mangrove prop roots form impenetrable barriers that create a rich and safe habitat for fish and birds.

deeper channels also host stands of flat bladed Eelgrass (*Zostera marina*), which also carpet many of the shallow areas of the lagoon interior where sufficient sunlight may penetrate the water to support its growth.

By far the most conspicuous and impressive of the tidal plant community are the mangroves, dominated by the Red mangrove (*Rhizophora mangle*) and the White Mangrove (*Laguncularia racemosa*). Laguna San Ignacio and nearby Punta Abreojos are the northernmost limit to the range of these mangroves along the Pacific coast of Baja California, while the warmer waters of the Gulf of California support mangroves as far north as Bahia de los Angeles. These large woody plants are specialized to grow in the silty mud of tidal lagoons and estuaries, forming tidal swamp forests that in some parts of the world may grow 30 m or taller. In San Ignacio they rarely exceed 3 m but form thick impenetrable thickets in many locations around the lagoon's shores that provide exclusive habitat for marine invertebrates, fish, and many of the marine birds especially the herons and egrets.

The Red Mangrove's seeds germinate within a pointed pod-shaped fruit that develops on the plant, and drop off into the mud as living little plants ready to send out roots where they land, or because they float, they may be carried by the tides to other areas where they may establish new plants, and over time en-

Young Red Mangrove seedlings rapidly sprout prop roots and leaves and begin to establish a new plant, thereby expanding the mangrove marsh.

Reddish Egrets (*top*), Great Egrets (*middle*), White Ibises (*bottom*), and other species of wading birds are common in the Mangroves.

tire new marshes. The characteristic long green pods or "fruit" of the Red Mangrove are frequently discovered floating in the outgoing tides, or littering the drift lines along the lagoon's beaches. The leaves are evergreen and are found on the plants above the high water tide line, and provide excellent nesting platforms for birds. Below its green leaves the red mangrove are a maze of crossing prop-roots that anchor the plants in the mud and support the thick green foliage above. These prop-roots also are the primary avenue for the plants to receive oxygen and nutrients from the mud and seawater when submerged. Small oysters are often found growing on the prop-roots, where they filter plankton from the sea water when submerged.

White Mangroves are usually found around the margins of Red Mangrove marshes in Laguna San Ignacio, and while similar, the White Mangrove grows as a bushy shrub that sends out horizontal roots that spread under the surface of the mud and sand. These roots send out vertical, stout, erect ventilator or "air-roots" through which the plant receives oxygen. Small encrusting barnacles grow on and in these air-roots. The White Mangrove's flowers are small whitish clusters that produce 1–2 cm long fruits, which contain football shaped seeds that also sprout while still on the mother plant, and that float to help disperse the plants with the tides.

Mangroves as viewed from the air.

5 *Friendly Whales*

I T WAS THE WINTER of 1976, a year before we began our studies in Laguna San Ignacio, that we first heard reports of "friendly" or "curious" gray whales—whales
that approached whale-watching skiffs in Laguna San Ignacio and allowed people
to pet them. Eyewitness reports and pictures of "Nacho" the first reported friendly
whale of Laguna San Ignacio appeared in the San Diego papers, and fueled our
curiosity. The possibility of filming this behavior caught the attention of television producer Nic Noxin who was developing a documentary on great whales and
whale researchers for National Geographic television. In January 1977 he sent photographers Bill Weaver and Ken Nelson with us to the lagoon to be there when the
friendly whales made their appearance. But it took awhile. For weeks we went out
every day and offered ourselves to the whales . . . but no luck. They seemed little
interested in our small boat. Then, late one February afternoon off Punta Piedra
a juvenile whale swam under Bill and Ken's boat and began rubbing against it. As
Mary Lou and I approached, the whale submerged, and we waited. Lou donned
her face mask and stuck her head underwater to try to spot the animal. Her journal
entry says it all:

Mary Lou and "Gracie" meet for the first time in 1977.

"There, less than an arm's length away, above the gape of the mouth, was the large brown eye of the whale, staring directly back at me and following my every move as I reached toward it with my outstretched hand. Her friendly behavior was somewhat amazing and her movements underwater were graceful beyond description."

A good look at the whale's underside revealed that she was a female, and at approximately 7 m long, a juvenile with distinctive linear white scars on her head. In the next few weeks this particular whale would make the rounds to whale watching skiffs and delight the passengers with her antics. The collective whale watching community named the whale "Amazing Grace" or "Gracie" for short, and she had a multitude of fans. Gracie was amazing for many reasons.

Even in 1977 we were not certain what type of reception we would get from the whales of Laguna San Ignacio. But it was Amazing Grace, likely more curious about the small boat than by "friendliness" in the human sense, who first indicated we would be welcome as long as we came in peace. Gracie readily adopted us and our 4-meter inflatable boat as her personal toy. Using her head, she would lift us out of the water only to have our boat slide off the tip of her snout to swirl around her in circles. We felt like a big rubber duck in the bathtub with a ten-ton playmate. If we drifted into shallow water, she would swim under the boat and, lifting it slightly with her head, carry it and ourselves back into

Mary Lou and Gayle entertain Amazing Grace.

deep water to continue to play. Rolling under the boat, she would turn belly up with her flippers sticking three to four feet out of the water on either side of the craft, then lift us clear off the surface of the lagoon, perched high and dry on her chest between her massive flippers. At other times Gracie would submerge beneath us and release a tremendous blast of air that boiled to the surface in a giant Jacuzzi of white water that engulfed us and the boat. After such gymnastics Gracie would often lie quietly along side the boat to be rubbed. We obliged her with a vigorous massage along her back, head, and ribs, while she opened her mouth to display huge fringed curtains of creamy white baleen plates.

That first winter we learned that Gracie was the exception rather than the rule among gray whales. The majority of whales either ignored or avoided human observers. It was clear—"friendly" whales find you; you don't find them. Moreover, some friendly whales soon lost their timid ways and grew rambunctious. Play with such a large animal can be hard on both boat and observer, and we were fortunate to crack only a few boat floorboards and no ribs during these encounters.

Unfortunately, more than one friendly whale nudged a boat with such enthusiasm that passengers were knocked overboard and even injured when falling within their boats. One mischievous individual soon became known as "Bopper" for the severe blows it delivered to the bottoms of whale watching skiffs. We didn't like to spend a lot of time with Bopper because Bopper got a real thrill out of coming up under the boat and giving it a good whack. We learned to avoid and even run from that whale!

Things had to be kept in perspective. Working in four-meter long boats with whales three times that long and seventy times more massive was always something to take seriously. They're big and they could quite easily do some damage inadvertently. While we never had any truly aggressive encounters with them, there were a couple of accidents when boats were traveling along and a whale came up unannounced underneath the moving boats, and the boats went over. When we first came to the lagoon we puzzled why the fishermen would bang their oars or use clubs to pound on the bottoms of their boats while they transited over deep water. Later we learned that they believed the whales would hear and avoid the banging noise. Fortunately, no one was ever seriously hurt in San Ignacio during our stay. But across from Punta Piedra were two crosses in the dunes apparently marking the graves of two fishermen that died after a collision with a whale; a reminder that we always needed to pay attention when traveling on the water.

We learned to use the outboard motor to elicit sounds from whales, a sort of primitive inter-species dialogue. We noted that friendly whales generally approached our skiff from behind and underneath, and pointed themselves right at the idling outboard engine. By revving the outboard engine we could get them to "trumpet" blow below the surface, which produced a "bellow" or low rumbling sounds in response. Time and time again they produced quite a bit of sound with those big bubble bursts. They'd blast, we'd rev the engine and they'd blast again. We'd get this kind of rapport going back and forth.

We also learned if we shut the engine off, the whales would leave the boat, and abandon us. Re-starting the engine often brought them back for more attention. At times we couldn't avoid them, like in the middle of a weekly survey. More than once our whale counting was interrupted by a friendly that insisted we stop and pay it attention. Who's to argue with a 30-ton animal that wants attention? What was originally a rare phenomenon in 1977, became almost routine by 1982 as "friendly" behavior seemed to spread to more and more of the whales wintering in the lagoon, and involved single animals, groups of juveniles, and mother-calf pairs alike.

Our colleague Marilyn Dahlheim recorded and analyzed gray whale vocalizations in the lagoon. She described a variety of sounds, including clicks, rasps, the "bong" like that from a huge Chinese gong, snorts, moans, grunts, low-pitched roars, and metallic "bloink bloink" sounds similar to the sound of percolating coffee. By artificially broadcasting sounds underwater, Marilyn discovered that gray whales grew silent when they heard killer whale calls, or sounds not normally associated with the lagoon habitat. This "silent running" no doubt had survival value if they did not know if such sounds represented a threat or not!

Gray whales will frequently swim close and "spyhop" next to the large whale watching excursion vessels that visit the lagoon.

A gray whale takes interest in the warm generator cooling water coming out of the transom of *M/V Spirit of Adventure*. The warm stream contrasting with the cool lagoon water apparently provided the whale with a pleasant experience. When the on-line generator was switched from the starboard to the port set, the whale also moved to the other side. Photo: Pieter Folkens

Whether by intention or inadvertence, we wondered if the whale-watchers posed any threat to the whales? When we began our study in 1977, "friendly" whales were a rare occurrence. At the time "friendly" whales were a relatively new phenomenon which had caught the whale-watching operators off guard. In 1981 there were twenty-eight whale-watching excursions that visited the lagoon and twenty-six of these encountered friendly whales, allowing nearly seven hundred passengers to experience and pet them. The next year people on thirty trips repeatedly interacted with friendly gray whales. Reports of such behavior were beginning to come from other Baja breeding lagoons and elsewhere in the gray whales' range, including off Vancouver Island, British Columbia. Perhaps they "learned" the behavior in Laguna San Ignacio and took it with them on their migration?

The growing number of "friendly" whales suggested to us that these animals were becoming accustomed to whale-watchers in the lagoon. Mother whales that freely approach whale-watching boats and allow their calves to interact with people must not see these boats and their human occupants as a threat. We surmised that today's gray whales have never been harassed by whalers or whale-watchers, and are therefore not conditioned to avoid the advances of small skiffs. In contrast, the whales appear comfortable enough around the boats to allow their natural curiosity to show. They seem especially interested in the low frequency "purring" of the outboard motors and often approach the boats from the stern to investigate them. We also concluded at the time that the level of whale-watching in Laguna San Ignacio had no adverse biological effect on the animals as many identifiable individuals returned each year and repeated their curious behavior. Some of these mother whales would routinely approach us and allow their calves to swim around and rub against our boat while they caught a cat nap for a few minutes.

We were pleased to report that at this time, whale watching and "friendly" whale encounters continue in Laguna San Ignacio, and the whales' have not abandoned the area. In the 1990s a comprehensive management plan for whale-watching eco-tourism was developed for Laguna San Ignacio to manage the number of tour-operators and boats on the water at any one time. The Lower lagoon nearest the ocean was designated as the official whale-watching zone, while the Middle and Upper Lagoon areas were closed to excursion boats, thereby creating a sanctuary for the whales and their calves. The management plan and the Eco-Tourism Operators Association that enforce the whale-watching zone are providing non-competitive access to the whales for all to come and see them.

A gray whale calf receives a rubdown from whale watchers in 1978.

Gilmore's Lagoon

A full moon announced the spring tides, which in Laguna San Ignacio results in a 3-meter difference from high to low tide every six hours or so. The high spring tides brought flood tides that surged over the beach lines and flooded the extremities of the salt marshes that ring the lagoon's shores. It also made usually shallow channels passable for our flat-bottom inflatable boat. And, if the high spring tide occurred at mid-day, it was an ideal time to explore.

"I don't know what is back there" Ray Gilmore pondered as we scanned his chart of the lagoon. "You can't see beyond the mangrove line from the main channel," he stated, "one winter a skiff driver followed a channel behind Isla Abroa, but couldn't get any further. Too shallow." On our copy of Ray's map he'd drawn in "Back Lagoon" in pencil over a large blank portion of the map. Our satellite photograph indicated that there was a sizable body of water to the southeast behind Punta Piedra and Isla Abroa, and we had occasioned to follow the deepest channel back behind these areas, only to confirm water too shallow for our boat to navigate. But with a spring high tide at mid-day, it might just be passable.

Ray Gilmore, Mary Lou, and Steven in 1980. Photo: Gayle Dana

At dawn the spring incoming tide was running. We hastily loaded the inflatable boat with full gas cans, water bottles, a couple of days provisions, cameras and film. After writing a note of our whereabouts to the neighbors, we zipped up the tents and were off. We headed southeast down the narrows between Punta Piedras and Isla Abroa. Normally this was too shallow to pass, but the running tide had filled it sufficiently for us to skim through the shallowest part. Once past the narrows the back lagoon opened into a vast basin of sinuous channels, shallow sand bars and mud flats that lie behind Isla Ana. Navigating through these was a real chore. Often to make headway to the south, we had to follow a winding channel to the north until it merged into another, and another. The rising tide was helping us by flooding the shallows.

We made our way along the eastern shore of Isla Ana and finally came to its southern most point where we discovered a deep channel that opened to the sea. We'd found a second entrance to the lagoon system, complete with sand bars and breaking surf. And, of course, a couple of gray whales were moving in and out of the surf. Unfortunately, once inside the breakers, there was little to offer the whales in the way of water sufficiently deep for them. Less than a few kilometers inside this second entrance the water became shallow and divided into the maze of narrow channels and flats we followed to get here.

We went ashore just inside the point. After securing the boat we hiked across the point to the ocean side of the Isla Ana. The dunes were covered with thin Cordgrass (*Spartina foliosa*) and creepers of Sand Verbena (*Abronia gracilis*) separated by low areas dominated by Pickleweed (*Salicornia virginica*) and Salt Cedar (*Monanthochloe littoralis*). The flats that separated the dunes from the back

Coyotes patrol the lagoon shores at low tide looking for stranded birds and digging up "hatchet" clams to eat.

lagoon were in the process of being flooded by the rising tide as we made our way to the ocean. Upon arriving at the shore, we found ourselves standing on a ridge of Pismo clam shells (*Tivela stultorum*) layered on top of each other to a height of 2 meters or more. Scattered among the dunes we discovered numerous "tun" shells (*Malea ringens*). Long abandoned by their occupants, these turban-like shells were the size of coconuts and bleached white by months under the sun and polished by the wind. Along the tide line we found sand dollars larger than our hands along with numerous cone shells of unknown origin.

About half way down the length of the island we encountered about seventy California sea lions (*Zalophus californianius*) hauled out on the beach and sunning themselves on this warm February afternoon. We watched them for some time from behind the dunes. They all appeared to be adults, mostly females. Periodically one or two would leave the group and lumber down to the surf and disappear in the waves, as others would emerge from the surf and flop up onto the sand to sleep.

As we made our way along the beach walking north we began to find bits and pieces of wreckage from some unfortunate vessel. Bits of plywood, fiberglass and other remnants of a boat were scattered over a mile of beach among the natural rubbish in the sand. Then we came upon the hull of the vessel, a sailboat buried in the sand. From the looks of the remains it had burned and broken up in the surf when washed ashore. Later we learned that a few years earlier the vessel had wrecked on that outer beach, and the survivors had wandered inland to be rescued by local fishermen.

California sea lions frequent the lagoon during the winter, and some haul out on the shores of the islands in the interior of the lagoon in summer.

Mindful of the tide that would be reversing its rise in a few hours, we made it back to our boat and launched again into the lower portion of the back lagoon. We made our way across to the eastern shore, south of the "second entrance" and encountered small islands covered with red mangroves. Along the shore were more dunes and shell middens indicating ancient camp sites from long ago. On examination Mary Lou and Mike discovered a few arrowheads along with numerous flakes of black obsidian glass scattered among the ancient clam and oyster shells that marked the former encampments. Our southward progress was halted when we ran out of lagoon. We returned northward to spend the night at an abandoned seasonal fish camp we had passed earlier in the day. As the spring high tide reverted to the spring low tide it exposed miles of mudflats and eelgrass. We gathered scallops and a few clams as the sun was setting. That night we dined on fresh shellfish and noodles, and were serenaded by chorusing bands of coyotes that roamed the desert and shore searching for their dinners.

At dawn we were awakened by Mike yelling at the top of his lungs "Hey, bring that back here!" To ward off the chill of the wind, he had slept with his knit cap on. Apparently a curious coyote had found the scent of the cap too intriguing and had snatched it off Mike's head. In a flash Mike was up and running after the thief shouting and waving his arms. And, the coyote dropped the hat in his retreat. Just as well we were all up, as we needed to make our way back to the main lagoon and we knew that the next day's high tide would come an hour later and would be not quite as high as before.

All along the trip back to Punta Piedra we used our compass to take bearings on any noteworthy landmark and feature. Back at camp we calculated positions for these various features along the shores and, bit-by-bit, we drew in rough boundaries for the back lagoon. From these sketches and a recent satellite photograph we added the shoreline of the back lagoon to Ray's map. It was only fitting henceforth to refer to this area as "Gilmore's Lagoon." Years later we would learn that the local name of this body of water is "Estero de la Pitaya."

Banditos Negros

On several occasions we returned to camp to find our garbage scattered about. We'd go away for a couple of hours and come back and think that somebody had looted us. Ravens working in pairs were the culprits. So we had to go through elaborate procedures to raven-proof the camp. Despite our efforts, they would undo everything. They'd turn over stoves, empty trash bins, tear open bags, and scatter things around. Enter Radar or "Ray-Dog", a one year old Labrador retriever that spent a number of winters with us at the lagoon.

It was my day in camp. Lulu, Gayle and Eagle-Eye were out conducting the weekly whale survey. I was sitting outside our main tent sipping coffee while reading through the mail that had arrived the day before by whale-watching boat. There they were. Two ravens had landed on the table next to the camp stove. In a flash, Radar was after them barking. Both birds took off but flew close to the ground with Radar in hot pursuit. Ah, quiet again, or so I thought. A minute or two later here came the birds with Radar running full out a few meters behind. Through the yard between the tents and out past the tower they

Ravens are "banditos" of the desert, never missing an opportunity to get into mischief.

went. Back and forth they went across the camp. All the while the birds stayed about a meter off the ground leading the dog a meter or two behind.

This went on for about 20 minutes before Radar gave up the chase and collapsed at my feet panting. Both birds now resumed their perch on the camp table, and the exhausted "Ray-Dog" could care less. They were all quite hilarious. I gave him some water and few treats to soothe his injured pride as the camp guard dog. "How about some fishing Ray-Dog?" I said. "We should have dinner ready when the crew gets home this afternoon." Fishing, now that was something he could get into. Forget the ravens. Off we went to the "refrigerator", the mangrove channel at the east end of the island that reliably produced fish, even at low tide. On the way Ray-Dog chased no less than a dozen lizards. He didn't catch a single one, but who's counting?

Bathing with Sharks

Bathing in the sea is one of the most invigorating experiences one can imagine. A dip in the cool brine then a blow dry in the desert wind always did wonders for the skin, let alone the soul. We didn't think much of waiting until there was a good high tide, and diving off a convenient rock into the lagoon channel that wrapped itself around Punta Piedra. That is until one day when Mary Lou nearly provided a meal for a fish. Lulu was splashing about like a sea otter in chest-deep water, rinsing the shampoo out of her hair. She turned around to look into the sunset and as the water cleared from her eyes they focused on a dorsal fin headed her way. "Ah, a bottlenose dolphin coming to play" she first thought. Dolphins frequently followed the returning tide onto the mud flats to chase fish in the mangroves. But this dorsal fin, straight and stable, was followed by a tail fin, zigzagging sinuously back and forth along the surface.

I heard her scream and ran to the edge of the point to find Lulu standing on a rock shivering in the wind. Momentarily I was joined by Mike who immediately noted the shark swimming about where Mary Lou had been swimming. "Hammerhead" spoke Mike, "A big one, maybe about 12 feet judging from the distance between its fins." The shark spent about fifteen minutes cruising around looking for her, thrashing the water, swimming, until it finally gave up and left. "I thought it was a dolphin" shivered Lulu, "It came within two meters of its intended meal; me!" It was pretty scary. After that we all took baths together, or at least in teams of two, someone sitting up on the rocks watching while the other person splashed around.

Large aggressive sharks abound in Laguna San Ignacio. This Bull shark was caught by local fishermen near the entrance of the lagoon.

The local fishermen caught several sharks that winter, mostly bull sharks (*Carcharihinus leucas*) in the 3-meter range, and the occasional mako (*Carcharihinus mako*) shark was also taken. While "hooka" diving for lobster and scallops in the lagoon's rocky bottom the fishermen recounted instances where sharks had bothered them. One fellow proudly showed us the characteristic curved pattern of tooth scars across his shoulder where one had grabbed him. Yes, there were sharks in the lagoon, and some were big.

To Feed or Not to Feed

Over and over again whale watchers and naturalists visiting the lagoon questioned us about the whales winter feeding habits. The general knowledge of the day suggested that gray whales fasted during the winter when they were giving birth to their calves and mating. But the debate went on. "Did they feed while in the lagoons?" "Was there food for gray whales?" There seemed to be plenty of bait and small fish. The tremendous primary production of the lagoon's waters supported vast populations of clams and scallops. In the deeper waters were groupers, bass, lobsters and other species which supported the local fishing cooperatives. But what about the whales?

Occasionally we observed what appeared to be "mud plumes," characteristic clouds of mud created when gray whales bring mouthfuls of bottom sediments to the surface and filter their prey through their baleen. We'd also spent hours watching gray whales orient themselves into the falling tides and repeatedly spy-hopping with mouths full of water, sometimes laden with sand as it spilled from their mouths. We even saw and photographed a few whales skimming floating windrows of eel grass from the surface with their mouths open. But did these observations constitute serious feeding, or just "tasting"

Mary Lou and Steven prepare to dive in search of whale food.

Gray whales will headout and distend the throat with mouthfuls of muddy sandy water. Are they feeding? If so, on what?

what the lagoon offered. So, we set out to find out what food the lagoon might offer the whales.

One winter we rounded up as many scuba tanks as we could and began a systematic series of dives in search of gray whale food. The "scientific" knowledge of the day suggested that gray whales fed on dense beds of tube building amphipods that cover the sea floor in areas of the Bering and Chukchi Seas. They were also known to suck up swarming mycid amphipods (shrimp) over rocky bottoms in the Gulf of Alaska, and to strain ghost shrimp out of the mud in the portions of the Pacific Northwest. Armed with our sophisticated scientific bottom coring device (a 1-gallon coffee can with both ends cut out) and a set of brass sieves, Mary Lou and I began our assaults on the lagoon's benthic terrain. Dive after dive, can after can of mud and sand was cored from the bottom and filtered. Each time the results were mostly the same—rocks, pebbles, bits

Gray whales are often seen skimming eel grass and other plants off the water's surface.

of shells, and some eel grass. We did confirm that as you moved into the interior of the lagoon from the entrance, the bottom sediments transitioned from well mixed and well washed sands and rocks to silt and muddy bottom sediments. There was not much else to be found.

Diving these areas was never, ever relaxed. Our efforts were constrained by short periods during a slack tide. Any other time was like diving in a wind tunnel. The visibility was generally poor, especially when we began to dig around. And this made it difficult to look out for the large sharks we knew were present.

Once again, we attracted the attention of our fishermen neighbors. One afternoon Ramon, his wife, and two girls motored up and asked "Diving for gold? See any sharks?" After all what else would we be doing, right? After a lengthy explanation of the reason for our exploring the bottom, we received a polite and approving nod. Ramon and family turned and headed back to their home. Word soon spread through the community that Maria Louisa was SCUBA diving in the lagoon, something that was generally done only by the men. Shortly thereafter at a pot-luck social event hosted at one of the local ranches, Mary Lou was confronted by several young women that wanted to hear all about her diving exploits. Not only did she drive boats (another exclusively male activity), she was a marine scientist and diver. Lulu became quite the celebrity as time went along. Years later we learned that a number of the young people that we knew at the lagoon, perhaps inspired by "Maria Louisa," went on to become marine biologists and divers.

An adult whales lunges with a mouthful of muddy water.

A subadult gray whale makes an unusual backwards lunge. Water can be seen escaping from the gape of the mouth. Photo: Sergio Martinez.

6

Captain Eddie and the Queen

WHILE WE DIDN'T find fields of gray whale prey on the bottom, our season of diving did give us a look at yet another side of La Laguna. In front of Punta Piedra is a deep area where the sport fishing vessels carrying whale watchers liked to anchor because the rocky bottom was firm and minimized their chances of dragging anchor during the frequent strong winds and falling tides. There was one tricky side to this practice. Each time the tide changed direction 180 degrees, the boats would wrap their anchor chains around the rocks and occasionally they couldn't get them back.

Our good friend Eddie McQuen skipper of the "Pacific Queen" found himself in this predicament one winter day. The Queen had arrived the previous day while we were up lagoon conducting a survey. She had provisions and mail for us, and when Eddie called on the radio the next morning he asked if we had our SCUBA gear. "Why?" I asked. He explained the previous night

Captain Eddie McQuen's Pacific Queen.

the wind had changed and their anchor was wrapped around the rocks and wouldn't budge. Could we dive down and free it? Sure, we would give it try. Slack tide was at mid-day and that would be the best opportunity to avoid the strong water currents. When we arrived at the Pacific Queen, Eddie handed me a 6-ft long prybar and a Styrofoam coffee cup. He then told me, "Once you are in the water I'll move the boat up to slack the chain. Use the bar to free it from the rocks. Once it's free, get clear and let go of the coffee cup. When I see the cup I'll begin to pull in the chain." This sounded reasonable and, after knowing Eddie for a number of years, we had the utmost confidence in him and his abilities. Over the side Lulu and I went, following the Queen's anchor chain to the bottom.

On the bottom we could see we were in a field of huge boulders, some 4-meters or taller and swept clean by the strong currents that ran through this portion of the lagoon. Perched on the rocks were yellow sea fans and anemones. Schools of silvery fish and groupers hovered in the shadows of the rock outcroppings. Well, the good news was that we found the anchor reasonably clear, but the bad news was that during the night the chain had sawed its way into the side of a huge rock. With the chain slackened, Mary Lou and I worked it back and forth and slowly began to extract the chain from the groove it had worn deep into the rock. Then with the pry bar we managed to leverage it free. We then spent several minutes rearranging the anchor chain on the bottom so it would rise freely. Once we were clear I let go of the foam coffee cup. Eddie pulled up his chain and anchor and re-located the Queen.

We spent our remaining air further exploring this boulder field. This was a part of our front yard that we were seeing for the first time. We startled a sea turtle that shot out from under a ledge and disappeared in the murky water. And there were lobsters—big ones! The strong currents prevented the fishermen from setting their traps here, and so we saw some of the largest lobsters ever in between the rocks and ledges. I was looking for something. I reasoned that other ships probably anchored here for the same reasons boats do today, and there might be additional anchors down here. Some belonging to whalers and perhaps dated from Scammon's time, who knows? But my archeological yearnings would have to wait for another time as our air supply was depleted and the tide was beginning to run strong.

The shallow lagoon entrance is surrounded by pounding surf at all stages of the tide.

Surfing Whales

We had been kept off the water for three days during a prolonged rainy and windy storm. Yes, it does rain in the desert, and often Baja's winter storms deluge the area to the point where the few roads become impassable rivers of mud. First, torrential rains fell and turned the powder-dry soil on Punta Piedra into slippery red mud. Then the winds blew hard enough to pull the tent stakes out of the mud and collapse them down. This usually happened in the middle of the night. With cabin fever running high, the storm finally passed on the fourth day and the subsequent morning brought flat calm conditions with a cool overcast skies. Within moments we had our gear in the boat and sped toward the entrance of the lagoon to begin a whale survey. With the storm and other responsibilities it had been over a week since we conducted a count, and being near to the peak whale season, it was critical that we closely monitored the number of whales entering the lagoon.

The tide was still falling as we motored along the edge of the sand bars toward the entrance to avoid running into any whales. Traveling the edge over the shallows was a trick we learned from the local fishermen when they needed to get somewhere quickly and wanted to avoid the whales in deeper water. A few kilometers or so from the entrance we turned into the main channel and began to cross deep water. Mary Lou and Eagle began staring at the water over the side of the boat on the lookout for whales. "Wait, wait, hold up, hold up" Eagle shouted. "What are all those white things? As I slowed the boat Lou exclaimed "those are white clam shells on the bottom, but we are 20 meters of water!" Almost four days without sun had slowed the continuous plankton bloom that normally turned the lagoon's water soupy green, and now with the incoming tide, cold clear water recently up-welled from offshore began to flow over the entrance sandbars and fill the lagoon. Now we could see the bottom of the main channel, for the first and the only time during our five winters at Laguna San Ignacio. About then, we saw the first whale, underwater, and all of it! Not just the flukes or the head, but the animal's entire body passed slowly under us as it swam up lagoon from the entrance. I shut off the engine and we just sat there watching the whale swim underwater until it surfaced to blow and was gone.

We were on our mark at the entrance just inside the breakers, ready to start the survey. It was flat calm, incoming tide, and the only sound was a low power-ful rumble from the storm-generated breakers pounding the sandbars at the la-goon entrance to the west. All three of us looked at each other. "The conditions are perfect" someone said. "We might never get this chance again. If anything goes wrong, the tide will push us back into the lagoon rather than out to sea." A moment later I started the outboard and, abandoning all thought of the whale survey, we began to navigate the meandering channels that ran like streams through the delta of sand bars and shoals that made up the entrance of the la-goon. The larger channels were a good 30 to 40 meters across and bordered by shallows covered by only a few meters of water. As we watched, huge emerald green swells loomed up from the ocean's surface, feathered at their tops by the offshore breeze and began to spill over themselves creating mountains of white foam pounding the shallows.

A mother whale and her calf swim under the author's boat.

The scene was surrealistic. Safe in the deep water of the channel, we were surrounded by breaking combers that made tremendous noise and the air was an aerosol of sea spray glistening in the morning rays of sun that were now piercing the overcast sky. Slowly motoring along we began to see whales within the channel as they swam in from outside. As we watched another huge 10 to 12 foot swell lurch up over the shallows we were astounded to see a gray whale in it. The whale then began to kick its flukes as it rose and began sliding down the face of the breaking wave. "The whales are surfing, I don't believe this" I exclaimed! We'd seen coastal dolphins surf through breaking waves along the beach, and many times marveled at dolphins riding the stern wakes of boats. But this was a real first for us. For several minutes we watched as whales lurched down the face of the swells and rolled over in the pounding surf, flukes and fins flying.

Time stood still for us. The tide was now reaching flood stage. Soon the flow of water would reverse and we would be fighting our way upstream to get back into the lagoon. It was time to go. Once back inside we slowly made our way to camp, stopping along the way to photograph a few well-marked whales. The clear water was now gone as the changing tides stirred the sediments and mixed the lagoon water into its traditional soupy green color. The morning calm was now giving way to the desert winds from the east. As the wind rose the sound of the breakers faded and gave way to the cries of the gulls and terns that were now feeding on the bait carried by the tides as the shallows were draining. La Laguna had allowed us a glimpse of another of her secrets, and the whales too showed us another side of their nature: surfing. Now that was a story we enjoyed telling Ray Gilmore, during his next visit to the lagoon. "Well now", he puffed with his eyes wide and brows raised. "Tell me what you've seen?" "Ray" I said. "Sit down a minute. Have you ever seen whales surf?"

Running with the Whales

It was early April 1982. This late in the season whales in the upper lagoon were scarce, as are the whale-watching groups. But we wanted to make one final inspection before the season ended to see who was still in the lagoon. This day we had the lagoon to ourselves—there were few whales in the upper lagoon and no whale-watching boats visiting. Mary Lou and I had been out on the water all morning taking photographs of well marked whales in the upper lagoon nursery. We recognized a few whales from the distinctive white, orange, and other markings on their backs. By mid-day the wind was coming up from the east and slowly blowing us toward the entrance, and back toward our camp on Punta Piedra. As the wind picked up we sought shelter in a mangrove channel for some bird watching while we ate our lunch.

Upon emerging from the mangrove, we were pleased to find that the winds were abating in the late afternoon. We motored back into the center channel of the middle lagoon and slowly "trolled" for whales to photograph. Within minutes a female and calf announced their presence with powerful blow, and headed toward our skiff. As they approached we recognized Cabrilla and her calf Pinto. We had first seen them two months earlier when Pinto was quite young and noticeably smaller, dark grey-brown and floppy. He was now larger, fatter, covered with mottled spots, and completely in command of his swim-

The calf we named "Pinto" rolls under our inflatable boat to investigate the outboard motor.

ming abilities. As usual, he positioned himself astern of our boat, facing into the gentle propeller wash of the outboard engine and spinning around and around as we motored along. Lou put the outboard into neutral—the signal to get some friendly rubs. As we obliged our young friend, Cabrilla maintained station close by under and to one side of our boat. Her ten-meter length dwarfed our inflatable boat as we drifted with the tides toward the deep lower lagoon basin off Punta Piedra.

As we drifted into the deep water of the lower lagoon, with friendly mother and calf in tow, we could see dozens of whales facing into the falling tide as if large salmon swimming upstream. One after another they would rise to the surface to blow and sink back into the rushing current. Frequently one would surface vertically, "spyhopping" with its large head bobbing at the surface like a float, then slowly sinking and rolling to expose their blowholes for another breath before submerging. For over an hour we slowly motored among these giants, photographing their backs and marveling at their coordination and control. Repeatedly one or more would surface within arm's reach of our skiff, never once bumping us or acting in any threatening way. Actually, they seemed to ignore us, but we liked to think that we had been accepted by them as fellow lagoon dwellers, at least for the moment. Now and then one would spyhop with its throat grooves bulging with a mouth full of water. Once in the air, sea water would spill from the gape of the jaws. Were they feeding? On what? Or just tasting the water or flushing debris from their baleen. We were never quite sure.

It was April, and how Pinto had changed in three months! From a shy little calf, to a robust miniature adult that swam with confidence. As he swam around our boat for our final rubs, his mother remained off to one side, seeming impatient and uninterested in the game. After a few minutes, Cabrilla recalled her calf, and, smoothly lifting their flukes, both headed toward the lagoon entrance. We watched until they were out of sight, beyond the breakers, the surf, and the setting sun.

Departing Thoughts

After spending an entire winter with us, Gayle "Queen of the Western World" Dana had this to say about leaving the lagoon:

> *"4 April 1979: A very special time in my life; not many people can travel in their minds to blue sparkling waters, a glistening whale's back, a crying tern. Not many can dream of sitting on a rock in the desert under a full moon and lose themselves to the rhythm of a whale's breath on a still March night. Not many . . . The lagoon was up to its usual antics, with Murphy's Law in full force. A gale of wind, a northern. It must have taken us one and one-half hours to get to Francisco's. On the way up lagoon, I experienced a tribute that was so fitting and meant so much to me, for my last time on the lagoon. The north wind was creating big swells of green water, sprays of white spilling over the Avon and ourselves. Glancing to the south, into the glare of the sun, intensifying the powerful swells and dynamic spray, a whale, an adult, breached against the shore. I will never forget this whale and her calf. For ten minutes they paralleled us, the adult breaching once more, her mammoth, glistening body reaching skyward, her pectoral fins projecting outward, as if ready to take flight. They freight-trained as I*

Mother calf departing Laguna San Ignacio for the last time.

A spyhopping whale pauses to take a look at our boat as we passed.

never seen; first the cow pushed out and up into a graceful arc, surging with power, water whipping off the grey slick of her body. At the height of the arc, the calf would literally break through the sea beside its mother and come crashing down on its belly, not knowing its potential to arch its body into a smooth fluid motion like that of its mother."

This note in my journal captures the mood that accompanied the approach of April following each winter at the lagoon:

"March 31, 1977: Today we officially close our field station at Rocky Point. It was a nice calm sunny day, good for straightening up things and packing those items that we will not be using until we return to San Diego. It is hard for me to think about this experience ending, finally being over. After more than three months here, this lagoon has become a way of life. I've become accustomed to its weather and can feel and almost anticipate its moods. I've watched changes in its wildlife and once again become close to the moon and tides. You know that your days are numbered and you quietly watch them go by, while trying to live out as much as each day will allow. Thoughts of home and all that goes on there race through my mind. I do very much miss friends and home, but right now I am totally at peace in this place and I find it hard to rationalize leaving. In a way, I think I never will."

We took the old road out of the lagoon, across the mudflats and up into the hills to the east. It is old and rocky, but it passes through some very scenic areas. Climbing steeply out of the lagoon basin the road passes through arroyos filled with Cardon cactus and then date palms. Each valley is dotted with small ranchos cloaked in shade trees and separated by more desert. Children wave and elders tip their hats as you pass. Finally you arrive at the top of the mesa—a flat table top caped with volcanic alluvia. Here we stopped, got out of the VW bus and silently walked to the edge of the mesa to look out over the lagoon basin in which we had spent the last three months. Off to the west lay the blue-green lagoon disappearing into the haze and surrounded by white shores of salt encrusted mudflats. To think that while we were leaving, whales, birds, fish, wind, tides, mangroves, and all that we had come to know were still there living out another day.

7 *The Ecotourism Alternative*

W E COMPLETED OUR sixth and last year of field studies at Laguna San Ignacio in the spring of 1982, and eventually returned to graduate school to
complete our degrees. We set about analyzing and reporting on our findings
in journals and in books. While the lagoon was no longer in our daily lives it
continued to linger in the background, surfacing now and then in the context of
conversations on gray whale conservation and the politics of marine protected
areas. Life continued at the lagoon and many significant changes were beginning to evolve which would set the tone for the future of this unique place.

The establishment of the Vizcaino Biosphere Reserve in 1988 set the stage
for a new era of social and economic development in the Laguna San Ignacio
region. Biosphere reserves are intended to promote sustainable use of natural
resources and not just protection of an area. The Biosphere reserve includes:
"core areas" within which no development is permitted; "buffer zones" allows
regulated human activities that protect the core areas and are consistent with
conservation objectives; and "transition areas" in which rational exploration of
natural resource may take place in cooperation with local populations.

Whale-watchers and Eco-Tourism camp off Punta Piedras in 2007.

Ecotourism whale-watching in Laguna San Ignacio in 2006.

Under this framework, the local fishing cooperatives and businesses at Laguna San Ignacio organized to protect their interests in the lagoon's resources from non-resident users that were moving into the area and exploiting to depletion the lagoon's fish and shell-fish populations. Some fishing cooperatives began to experiment with whale-watching excursions which had proven so successful for the U.S. based companies. Using the United States whale watching excursions as examples, some local groups tried offering land-based whale-watching excursions, but these were only moderately successful. It was difficult to attract visitors from outside the local area, and to compete with the San Diego based excursion companies that had the resources for advertising and marketing their natural history excursions to the lagoon.

In 1993 then Mexico's President Carlos Salinas de Gortari implemented legislation that changed Mexico's laws regarding ownership of the public lands allowing the cooperatives to form "Eidos," whose members could collectively manage communal lands surrounding San Ignacio lagoon. These new rules also allowed the conversion of Ejido lands to private parcels, subject to only their owner's wishes for future development and exploitation. Some Ejido members converted their lands into private parcels to control future uses of their properties, rath-

Naturalists employed by the ecotourism companies provide an orientation to gray whales for the lagoon visitors.

Boat and land based excursions bring whale watchers to Laguna San Ignacio from all over the world.

er than to be subject to Ejido management. The resulting arrangement created competition between land owners and Ejido members for economic opportunities such as eco-tourism, fishing rights, and land development. Larger tour companies seeking to book excursions and facilities for their whale-watching clients began pitting one Ejido or land owner against the other offering eco-tourism services, which resulted in bidding-wars and conflicts over services and prices, and polarizing the lagoon's residents. The community needed a better way to develop their economic interests and to ensure the stabilization of their future.

By 2000 the local Ejido, Luis Echeverra Alvarez, and the ecotour companies agreed to create a new cooperative association, the "Asociación Rural de Interés Colectivo" (ARIC), and to work together to agree on standardizing the fees charged for ecotourism services. They elected a board of governors to represent all of their interests, and to act as a neutral party that would assure representation for all association members. They collectively developed and negotiated an ecotourism management plan with the federal authorities responsible for managing all lands within the Biosphere Reserve. While the management plan focused directly on ecotourism, it also addressed concerns of the local community, such as support services for ecotourism, waste management, recycling, public safety and human health, and education. Clearly the community's vision was to use the land responsibly and create a sustainable way to support their livelihood.

The ecotourism management plan established a number of operational conditions to provide equal access to the lagoon's recreational and ecotourism assets, while conserving and preserving the integrity of the lagoon ecosystem. The plan set limits for whale-watching excursions times (initially 90-min), and limits the number of whale-watching excursions that are allowed on the water each day. It established the "observation zone" where whale-watching excursions are permitted to operate, and closed areas so as not to overpopulate the lagoon with boats and noise. The inner two-thirds of the lagoon was set aside as a reserve or "sanctuary" for the gray whales, with only local fishermen and scientific researchers permitted to operate boats in this portion of the lagoon during the winter. Similarly, nets and other fishing gear that could entangle whales was permitted only during months when whales are not in residence.

The management plan developed by and adopted by the community established regular work schedules for employees of the companies, their break times, wages, etc. Records were kept of all whale-watch excursions to document and demonstrate compliance with the regulations of the Biosphere Reserve. An inspector was hired to monitor and enforce these self imposed rules by all operators. Annual workshops were implemented to review and discuss rules and regulations with all ecotour operators and boat operators, known as "pangueros." The management plan was presented to and endorsed by the authorities of the Biosphere Reserve, and thereby gave the members of the ARIC a single united voice to represent all of their interests to the government.

The community was now poised to support itself, and to support sustainable development with the Laguna San Ignacio wildlife area as its foundation. For the moment, La Laguna and its residents, human and non-human, were able to continue to live their lives as they had long before whale-watching came to the lagoon.

The success of ARIC reflects the dedication of the ecotourism operators, and the local residents of Ejido Luis Echeverría Alvarez to strive to be stewards of the "ecosystem," and to set an example of maintaining a balance between ecotourism, community development, and biological integrity of the lagoon. The prosperity of local business provides the economic incentive to preserve the lagoon habitat as a world class wildlife experience attracting visitors from every continent.

Thirty years ago most whale watchers arrived at Laguna San Ignacio on San Diego based sport fishing vessels that numbered only a few dozen trips each winter. Other than the few local families that fished and ranched at the lagoon, human visitation was sparse to say the least, and economic benefits to the locals from these whale-watching trips were minimal. Today, multitudes of visitors travel to Laguna San Ignacio each winter by boat, plane or over land to book excursions with the ecotourism companies, and to view gray whales from locally owned and operated "pangas" staffed by professional boat operators and naturalists. Others come to take kayak excursions into the mangrove marshes for a chance to view more than 200 species of waterfowl and marine birds that frequent the lagoon, or venture on mule-back into the Sierra de San Francisco, east of the lagoon, to view cave paintings and petroglyphs placed there by ancient societies as depictions of the wonders of their world.

And, as in the past, hundreds of gray whales continue to arrive at Laguna San Ignacio in January and remain in residence until April each year. These include the now famous "Friendly Whales" of Laguna San Ignacio, whose natural curiosity for humans in small boats continues to thrill and amaze all human visitors.

8 Salt Wars of the 1990s

IT WAS EARLY in 1994 the when Francisco "Pachico" Mayoral learned of plans by owners and operators of Exportadora del Sal (ESSA) and the Mitsubishi Corporation to build a $180 million solar-wind salt production facility at Laguna San Ignacio. Pachico and his family lived in a simple home where the road from the town of San Ignacio reached the eastern shore of the lagoon. Over the years he had made friends with generations of scientists and conservationists that visited and worked in Laguna San Ignacio and elsewhere throughout the Baja Peninsula. As a spokesperson for maintaining the unique character of the lagoons, Pachico's years of experience and insights into the Lagoon, its wildlife, and the need for its protection were invaluable. He provided copies of the plans for the salt production facility to conservationists Emily Young and Serge Dedina, and thus began a 5-year campaign to raise public awareness of the proposed industrial facility at the lagoon, and to recognize the potential for such a project to forever change the lagoon's ecosystem and affect all the wildlife that resided there.

Throughout the 1990s political and social wars raged over the proposed development of the industrial scale solar salt production facility in Laguna San Ignacio. While ESSA was behind the project, financial backing came from the Mitsubishi Corporation and the Mexican Government, which owned 49% and 51% of the company, respectively. ESSA's proposed plan was to build and operate an industrial solar powered salt production plant in Laguna San Ignacio, similar to their operation on the shores of Ojo de Liebre Lagoon in the town of Guerrero Negro to the north. The proposed design would utilize thousands of acres of natural salt flats in the desert north of the lagoon to create a vast network of shallow ponds for the evaporation of seawater. Seawater would be pumped from the lagoon into these evaporating ponds where the prevailing winds and relentless sun would concentrate the brine into industrial grade sea-salt, creating hundreds of square kilometers of snow-white, salt-harvesting fields. The evaporation process would also produce thousands of gallons each year of toxic brine waste products containing concentrated heavy metal-salts.

Once harvested, the salt would be transported to the lagoon's entrance where a 1 km long pier was to be built from the shore at Estero Coyote into Ballenas Bay to allow ocean freighters to load the salt and transport it to foreign markets. Such an operation would introduce shipping noise to the bay and the lagoon, create the potential for fuel spills, introduce massive trucks and salt harvesting equipment to the once undeveloped desert, and add another community of people that would place further demands on local water, electrical, and waste management services. When the proposed plan was examined by experts, the impact to wildlife of daily pumping millions of gallons of seawater from the lagoon could not be established

Solar salt evaporation ponds at Guerrero Negro, B.C.S.

or agreed upon. Perhaps the most lasting environmental concern would be the dramatic transformation of the desert landscape on the north side of the lagoon by huge tracts of man-made salt evaporation ponds and around the clock harvesting activities.

The magnitude of the proposed project at Laguna San Ignacio, and the development required to implement and operate it would change the landscape of the lagoon and surrounding region forever, and conflict with Mexico's efforts to legally establish the region as a special ecological reserve for whales and other species, and as a cultural heritage site. Mexico found itself in the awkward position of weighing the benefits and costs of development and permanent changes to the lagoon system, versus preserving this wilderness area for ecotourism, local fishing, and marine wildlife.

When word of Exportadora de Sal's plans to build a salt works project around Laguna San Ignacio reached the environmental community in Mexico, the Group of 100 reacted. The Group of 100 was led by Homero Aridjis, one of Mexico's most respected writers on the environment, poetry, literature and novels, and the Group of 100 is the most influential environmental organization and advocate for the environment in Mexcio. On January 21, 1995, Homero Aridjis published an article in the Mexico City independent daily newspaper "Reforma" criticizing the government of Mexico's handling of the salt works project, and outlining the importance of Laguna San Ignacio to gray whales and other marine life. Soon additional

Laguna San Ignacio without industrial salt production.

articles appeared in the Los Angeles Times, the New York Times, and the San Diego Union-Tribune newspapers. All this further activated the international media, and made people around the world aware of the potential threat facing Laguna San Ignacio and its gray whales.

Mexico's Ministry for the Environment, Natural Resources, and Fisheries (SEMARNAP) was the government agency responsible for matters dealing with the environment including gray whales. Previously in 1994 Mexico's President Ernesto Zedillo appointed Dr. Julia Carabias, an internationally respected biologist, to head SEMARNAP. On February 27, 1995 ESSA's initial environmental impact statement prepared for the salt production project was rejected by SEMARNAP on the grounds that the proposed project was "incompatible with the goals of conservation" of the Biosphere Reserve. In its decision SEMARNAP did agree to re-evaluate the project, if a new environmental impact statement prepared by ESSA addressed the relevant biological, social, and economic aspects of the proposed project. The public outcry in opposition to the saltworks project was becoming cautiously optimistic about the process set in motion to review the project, and hope that common sense would prevail on behalf of the gray whales and the environment.

In her opening address to the Mexican Society for Marine Mammalogy (SOMEMMA) in April 1995 in La Paz, Dr. Julia Carabias stated that "Science and not politics will determine whether the salt works is built." She was attempting

Sierra Santa Clara viewed from the south shore of Laguna San Ignacio at dawn.

to open a traditionally closed process of review for this and similar development projects in Mexico. Her intent was to set a precedent that subsequent environmental reviews should be objective, based on science, and take into account the views and interests of all affected constituents. She convened an International Scientific Committee to advise SEMARNAP on the Environmental Impact Assessment process for the proposed project. I was honored to be selected to serve on this "committee of experts" along with six additional distinguished international scientists. Our charge was to identify and describe the biological questions that were relevant to such a project and to examine the potential consequences to wildlife of changes to the Laguna San Ignacio ecosystem if this project were to go forward.

In February of 1996 the committee of experts held a day-long public hearing in La Paz, Baja California Sur, the first ever such meeting in Mexico to solicit public input for an environmental impact process. Following the public hearing, our committee made a site visit to both the ESSA salt production facility at Guerrero Negro, and Laguna San Ignacio. In the weeks that followed our committee developed a report on the "Biological Terms of Reference" for the Laguna San Ignacio salt works project. We presented this report to Dr. Carabias at a three hour meeting in Mexico City, where she informed us that we would be asked to review the second environmental impact assessment that ESSA was developing.

At that same time, prominent national and international environmental organizations formed the "Coalition to Save Laguna San Ignacio," and began a coordinated effort to bring the salt works project and the potential consequences for Laguna San Ignacio into the public arena for debate. Suddenly, San Ignacio's gray whales, the salt works project, and the development dilemma facing Mexico were beginning to make front page news around the world. The Coalition organized events that brought internationally recognized celebrities from film, television, conservation, and government to the lagoon for site visits. This included Mexico's President Zedillo and his family, who toured the lagoon, went whale-watching, and met some of the friendly whales up close and personal. Then on March 2, 2000, following almost five years of contentious public debate, Mexico's President Zedillo halted the San Ignacio salt works project stating:

> *"There are few places in the world like the Vizcaino Reserve…We're dealing with a unique place in the world both for the species that inhabit it, and for its natural beauty, which we should preserve."*

Mexico established gray whale sanctuaries in Laguna Ojo de Liebre and Laguna San Ignacio during the 1980s, and now President Zedillo's decision demonstrated Mexico's resolve and leadership for preserving wilderness areas for breeding gray whales. This time, however, it was clear that the Laguna San Ignacio reserve was intended to protect all the species that lived there, which included protecting the livelihood of its local people.

As a hedge against future development threats to the Laguna San Ignacio wetlands complex, in early 2003 a consortium of Mexican and international environmental groups formed the Laguna San Ignacio Conservation Alliance (the International Community Foundation, WILDCOAST, Pronatura Noroeste, and Natural Resources Defense Council). The Alliance pursued a multi-layered conservation plan aimed at protecting the health of the lagoon's mangroves, floodplains, mudflats, riparian areas, and coastal lands that support the ecological function of the lagoon, and ensure the protection of gray whale breeding grounds. Their goal was to put in place measures that would conserve and guide development in the areas surrounding the lagoon, and secure the lagoon's future as an ecologically healthy and functional marine protected area.

The legal reforms in Mexico in the 1990s gave the Ejidos the power to sell communal lands, and there was a very real threat that developers could offer to buy Ejido lands for private development. But the new laws also gave Ejidos the power to sell "conservation easements" that, if properly structured, could restrict development and prevent any development that was inconsistent with the mission of the Biosphere Reserve and the aspirations of the local community. The Alliance quietly worked with local landowners, the Ejidos, and the Mexican National Protected Area Commission (CONANP) to use conservation ease-

ments to conserve hundreds of thousands of acres of lagoon habitat and wetlands around Laguna San Ignacio. Taking advantage of the new and developing
laws on land conservation easements in Mexico, the Alliance launched a capital
campaign to raise funds to buy land conservation easements from the Ejidos
that owned lands around the Laguna San Ignacio wetlands complex. Contributions to the Alliance members by their supporters raised the capital which was
placed into an investment "Trust Account." The interest earned from this trust
account was reinvested back into the rural communities of Laguna San Ignacio
in return for a conservation easement over all of their communal use lands. It
was intended that by subsidizing conservation easements the local community
would not be under future pressure to sell their lands to foreign corporations,
or to agree to ill-conceived development projects.

In 2005, the Ejido Luis Echeverria Alvarez negotiated a conservation easement of 120,000 acres to protect their communally-owned lands in perpetuity;
in subsequent years, private landowners negotiated similar arrangements on an
additional 40,847 acres on the southern shore of the lagoon. Like the greater
Biosphere Reserve, these conservation easements contain development "zones"
within which specific activities and uses were permitted. Each year, these ease-

A salt barge loading at Guerrero Negro, a gray whale calving lagoon.

ments are monitored for conservation and development progress and if the conditions are met, a payment is made to a local nonprofit that supports community development projects and welfare of Ejido residents. This arrangement has been functioning well by providing support for the communities needs as well as for protecting the environment. This fundamental approach to achieve the goal of securing the future of the lagoon ecosystem was beginning to take shape, as summarized by Serge Dedina:

"For those who work in the developing world, conservation is as much about social justice as it is about protecting wildlife. Unless the social needs of rural people are met first, there will never be that much wildlife around to preserve."

Then, in 2010, a conservation management program was approved for 222,000 acres of federal lands along the northern shores of the lagoon. This is a precedent-setting agreement between CONANP and the conservation nonprofit, Pronatura that gives Pronatura full management authority on those lands, which overlap significantly with the previous lands and salt production concession to ESSA, and further advanced the conservation future for the lagoon.

The Laguna San Ignacio marine protected area was never intended to become a museum. Rather, like the larger Vizcaíno Biosphere Reserve, it is zoned to permit specific activities that provide the economic basis for the local communities, provided those activities can be conducted in accordance with the mandates and mission of the Biosphere Reserve, and maintain the biological integrity and productivity of the ecosystem. In the case of Laguna San Ignacio, local fishing cooperatives, eco-tourism associations, the community, and government officials evolved a partnership for conservation to sustain the unique nature of the lagoon and their own livelihoods.

Unquestionably, the gray whales were the champions for this larger need to preserve a unique marine habitat, on which all seasonal and permanent resident species depended. President Zedillo's decision was no doubt influenced by the then director of SEMARNAP. Dr. Carabias proved to be a courageous leader and dedicated proponent of a forward vision for economic development without sacrificing the conservation of wilderness areas in Mexico. Thanks to her efforts and the efforts of countless individuals and organizations, Laguna San Ignacio and its residents, human and non-human, will be able to continue to live their lives as they have, and future generations will come to appreciate something that man did not make, but had the wisdom not to change.

Children from the near-by town celebrate the tenth anniversary of the cancellation of the salt works with a special whale watch, including rainbows. Photo: Sergio Martinez.

March 2nd 2010 marked the tenth anniversary of the decision not to build the salt production plant at Laguna San Ignacio. To mark this occasion, many of the individuals and activists who worked hard to ensure the protection of La-guna San Ignacio traveled to the lagoon to celebrate the decision to protect the lagoon for future generations to enjoy. This reunion reaffirmed and rekindled the commitment of the local and extended international communities to sus-tain the viability of San Ignacio Lagoon as a habitat for gray whales and other marine wildlife, and in so doing continue to provide an economic basis for the ecotourism and fishing that sustain the local population. One of the highlights of this meeting was a day of whale-watching provided to the school children by the ecotourism companies and NGO organizations. When we visited the local schools, we were surprised to learn that many of the sons and daughters of the eco-tour operators had never been on the water to see the whales . Thus began an effort to coordinate a group whale-watching event for these young people. On the last day of the reunion, the ecotour companies drove their buses and vans to the schools, picked up more than 100 students and their instructors, and delivered them to Campo Cortez. There they were met by panga operators, loaded into the pangas, and went off to see the whales. For many this was the first time they had been on the water and seen whales close up. This was indeed a very special way to pass the conservation torch to the next generation.

9 The Future

The Resurrection of Lagoon Science

THE SALT WARS emphasized the reality that all protected wilderness areas are potential targets for future development, and served as a wake-up call for communities to actively voice and defend their opinions about the future of their own lands and livelihoods. From a scientific perspective, when asked to demonstrate the "value" of an undeveloped Laguna San Ignacio compared to a commercial industrial development, we found it challenging to articulate a cogent and convincing argument against the "economic value" of development.

As a research community, we scrambled to cobble together bits and pieces of field studies and research by previous investigators, historic records of wildlife in the region, and incomplete studies and reports to build the strongest biological argument we could to counter the proposed "benefits" from the development of the area. In the end, we felt we had not captured nor adequately characterized the biological reality of this wildlife area as a cultural and natural

Researchers conducting a gray whale abundance survey.

resource, and that our efforts to underscore its "value" as a natural resource were inadequate. Something needed to be done to build a body of scientific evidence on which to base a convincing argument in support of maintaining this wilderness area, and to fend off the next and likely inevitable assault by developers.

I returned to Laguna San Ignacio in the winter of 1996 at the invitation of my colleague Dr. Jorge Urbán R. and his scientific team from the Autonomous University of Baja California Sur (UABCS). Encouraged by the need for current information on the winter use of the lagoon by breeding gray whales resulting from the proposed ESSA salt production project, Jorge and his researchers from the Marine Mammal Research Program at the UABCS had resumed winter gray whale surveys in the lagoon after a fourteen year hiatus in scientific activity. I was asked to help design the survey plan, so that new information on the use of the lagoon by gray whales would be comparable with the whale abundance surveys that Mary Lou and I conducted during the late-1970s and early 1980s.

We first needed to re-construct our exact survey course from 16 years earlier using the various landmarks along the lagoon's shores and the surrounding hills that ringed the entire lagoon basin. I brought one of our original charts, a bit worse for wear but readable, to use as a guide for establishing the proper position of the survey track within the lagoon and noting places where the track turned. We recruited Pachico to drive the panga that first day we attempted the survey. After such a long absence I wasn't sure if I would remember all the landmarks, but once on the water, everything fell into place as if I had never left. As various landmarks lined up with the shores of the lagoon I directed Pachico

The author and the LSIESP field team conduct abundance surveys from a panga in Laguna San Ignacio.

The field laboratory at Laguna San Ignacio in 2008.

where and when to make a turn. In the meantime, Jorge's students entered our course and waypoints into a GPS unit, a new and effective technology we did not have in the 1980s. We now had an accurate record of the survey rout to navigate, and a reliable way to replicate the gray whale surveys from the past. As before, we used a survey speed of 11 km/hr to optimize the likelihood of seeing a submerged whale while the survey boat was passing through the lagoon, and minimizing the possibility of double counting the same whales.

I was somewhat anxious of what I would find having been away from the lagoon for so long. To my relief, I found the lagoon in good shape overall. The air and water were filled with whales, fish, birds, and whale-watchers. Whale-watching and desert ecology, not politics, were now the primary focus of international visitors. With ecotourism companies well in place, there was now an economic base for sustaining the community that would preserve the unique nature of the lagoon and its marine life for the enrichment of visitors and the benefit of the local residents, including the whales and other marine life.

One very real problem loomed over any future science programs at the lagoon: funding! With the end of the controversy over the salt production project, the funding for scientific research at the lagoon also ended. Without a controversy, well intentioned environmental organizations turned their attention to other pressing conservation issues. There was no sustained environmental monitoring program for the lagoon and its wildlife, and no means to provide a sense of the biological health of the lagoon and its tidal wetlands. So, in 2006 with our colleagues Jorge Urbán R., and Alejandro Gómez-Gallardo U. of the UABCS we developed and established the Laguna San Ignacio Ecosys-

Multi-disciplinary university researchers at the field laboratory.

tem Science Program (LSIESP) with the intent to provide systematic science based information on the wildlife in the lagoon and to assess the health of the surrounding ecosystem itself. Our plan was for university researchers to gather information on a suite of "ecosystem indicators" that represented a mix of physical parameters (e.g., sea temperature and salinity) and biological parameters that include a range of organisms representing various trophic levels (e.g., primary production, zooplankton, fish, turtles, migratory waterfowl, dolphin, and gray whales). To be meaningful, each component of the overall program would need to continue for a period of years to yield information sufficient to detect and describe trends in the wildlife and the lagoon ecosystem. Otherwise we would find ourselves with more bits and pieces of research, and no way to provide an overall evaluation of the lagoon ecosystem over time. This would require a longer term commitment on the part of funders, something that was rare in conservation science programs.

We intended the LSIESP's findings to be reported to the local community, schools, our academic colleagues, and Mexico's wildlife management agencies. In our vision we saw this ecosystem science program including outreach components to deliver relevant findings to the local community, and to involve them in the direction of the overall research program. As we began to circulate our proposal, we discovered to our delight and amazement, several non-government conservation organizations shared our vision and supported our "ecosystem approach" concept, and they generously provided funding to initiate the LSIESP in 2006.

We implemented LISESP by building on available historical information (when it was available), and implementing new studies where there had previously been none. We convinced our academic colleagues to bring their students to the lagoon, where we offered shared field facilities and support for conducting their various research programs. The overall goal was to document trends in the wildlife populations and their use of the lagoon's habitats over time. In this way we hoped to foster an understanding and appreciation of the complex dynamics between lagoon wildlife populations, the physical and biological environment within and outside the lagoon, and the human population that makes its livelihood from the lagoon either from eco-tourism or fishing.

To staff this multifaceted research program, we drew on the academic resources at UABCS and other universities within Mexico and abroad. The principal research force consists of Masters and Ph.D. level students, and collaborating researchers from Mexican and other universities. They contributed their specific expertise in a variety of subjects related to the lagoon and its ecology. These include experts in marine zoology, marine mammal biology, marine botany, biology, oceanography, and desert ecology (to name a few). By employing university students as researchers, the program provided opportunities for them to participate in applied wildlife conservation and field research,

R/V Rhachianectes and crew prepare for a day on the water.

while learning skills that would bolster their careers as wildlife conservation scientists. Research findings are disseminated in scientific publications, lay-person journals and articles, at professional scientific meetings, and through the program's Internet web-site at **www.lsiecosystem.org**.

With the help of Kuyima Ecotourismo we established a small field laboratory on the southern shore of the lagoon. It is within sight of the historic La

LSIESP researchers visit a local school in 2011.

Freidera whaling station from the days of captain Scammon. Our friend Mike Symons set up a solar and wind electrical generating system so the lab would have lights at night and the ability to charge our various electronics, cameras and computers. In addition to monitoring the gray whales that wintered in the lagoon, we attracted colleagues that brought their students to study the marine birds, underwater acoustics, and marine plants (including the vast eelgrass meadows that carpet the lagoon). Later, one of Pachico's sons, Ranulfo Mayoral (a fisherman raised at the lagoon and now an "eco-tour naturalist,") began studying green turtles that forage in the lagoon. Then he initiated the first ever survey to monitor the sea lions that occupy the islands in the northern portion of the lagoon during the summer.

With the help of other non-profit organizations we reached out to the local schools and began presenting programs on the lagoon's wildlife and conservation to the next generations of guardians of Laguna San Ignacio. Soon after these visits began and with the help of the ecotourism companies, classes of students were making field trips to the lagoon as part of their regular classroom curriculum.

In 2009 the Laguna San Ignacio Ecosystem Science Program became a project of The Ocean Foundation: a Washington, DC, based non-profit organization that promotes ocean conservation. The program began and continues to be supported entirely by non-government, non-profit organizations and foundations within Mexico and the United States, and from donations and gifts from individuals. To date, the Laguna San Ignacio Ecosystem Science Program is achieving its goal to provide science based information on the biological status of the lagoon and its wildlife. This aids in the evaluation of management efforts currently in place, and a means to evaluate future options. Through its outreach efforts and its website, the program is promoting social awareness and participation from within the community, and it has become a resource for environmental education in the local schools to ensure the future conservation of this unique marine protected area. And the new generations of marine conservation scientists are completing their university degrees and entering the wildlife science workforce in Mexico.

The Laguna San Ignacio gray whale research team in 1981.

The Science Mentors of Laguna San Ignacio

Steven L. Swartz has researched and published widely on gray whales and their breeding lagoons in Baja California. He served as a consultant to the Mexican government's Ministry for the Environment, Natural Resources, and Fisheries (SEMARNAP), and worked for the Ocean Conservancy (previously the Center for Environmental Education), the U.S. Marine Mammal Commission, the National Marine Fisheries Service, and the International Whaling Commission (IWC).

Mary Lou Jones in addition to conducting the first systematic studies of gray whales in Laguna San Ignacio, she undertook the most detailed bathymetric studies of the lagoon, the first multi-year evaluation of potential impact of whale-watching activities on whales in that lagoon, and published the first estimate of calving interval based on photo identifications. Her research on gray whales and other marine topics have appeared in numerous publications including the journal of the IWC's Scientific Committee, the National Geographic Society, the 2002 and 2009 editions of the Encyclopedia of Marine Mammals. She was the lead editor for and contributor to *The Gray Whale* (Academic Press, 1984).

Jorge Urbán R. is a professor of marine science and marine mammal biology at the Universidad Autónoma de Baja California Sur, La Paz, B.C.S., where he is the Coordinator of the Marine Mammal Research Program since 1988. He has led gray whale research in Baja since 1996. He has written more than fifty publications on marine mammals and marine conservation. He serves on the IUCN Cetacean Specialist Group, the Scientific Committee of the International Whaling Commission and is a past President of the Mexican Society for Marine Mammalogy (SOMEMMA).

Alejandro Gómez-Gallardo U. is on the teaching faculty of the Universidad Autónoma de Baja California Sur, La Paz, B.C.S., Mexico where he directs the department of marine science. His research and teaching interests include vertebrate anatomy, marine ecology, marine mammals and the interactions between whale and human activities. He is a past President of the Mexican Society for Marine Mammalogy (SOMEMMA).

Lingering Concerns

Over the decades, the eastern North Pacific population of the gray whale has increased to become relatively stable and is no longer in immediate danger of extinction. At least two gray whales have appeared in the Atlantic for the first time in perhaps two hundred years. Even so, the western North Pacific population remains in danger and treats continue to exist for the entire population.

One insidious threat is that of whales becoming entangled in derelict fishing gear (such as gill nets) and crab and lobster pots that form a nasty gauntlet along much of their near-shore migration route. In some places along the California and Oregon coasts, pots are place only a few dozen meters apart in areas gray whales are known to feed in the spring.

A common feeding behavior of gray whales involves turning to one side to pursue invertebrates on the bottom or mycids in the water column. If a crab pot line rising to the marker buoy at the surface is in the whale's path, that line may get caught crosswise in the whale's mouth. It can become stuck at the gape

This whale appeared in Laguna San Ignacio entangled with a crab line and buoy. It may have acquired the entanglement elsewhere and brought it into the lagoon.

This whale was inextricably stuck, grounded by a crab pot line for several days. It was successfully disentangled and is likely to survive. Photo: Pieter Folkens.

Specially trained Biosphere Reserve staff and researchers attempt to remove a buoy line from an entangled calf in Laguna San Ignacio.

Have you seen me? The two gray whales shown above are among the whales
disentangled by trained responders in recent years along the West Coast.

of the mouth. Trying to shake the gear loose often causes the line to become
wrapped around the pectoral fins, rendering the whale helpless to shed the gear.

In recent years, responses have been launched by members of the Vizcaino
Biosphere Reserve, researchers and conservationists working in Baja California
lagoons with favorable results. With funding provided by U.S. non-profit conservation organizations, disentanglement responders authorized by the U.S. National Marine Fisheries Service have conducted disentanglement training workshops in Mexico to help local responders develop the special skills necessary to
affect successful disentanglements. It is not an endeavor for the faint of heart.
Within Mexico's Biosphere Reserve, disentanglement efforts require official au-
thorization, appropriate training, and specialized equipment to attempt the safe
removal of lines and other fishing gear from whales.

When whales are disentangled, identification photos are obtained and
shared with LSIESP and researchers counting whales along the migration
route in the hopes that the formerly entangled whales will be identified in the
future and are seen again as participating members of the breeding population of gray whales in the lagoons. Such resightings will further justify the effort and expense required to continue disentangling programs going forward
all along the Pacific coast.

The gray whales' range includes many areas of extensive human development, corroded with economic and industrial activities. The whales' habits often result in conflicts with human activities and afford additional threats to gray whales throughout their geographic distribution. Ship collisions, coastal development, oil and gas exploration and development, exposure to pollution, low-frequency noise pollution from military and civilian sources, derelict fishing gear, and illegal whaling all confront gray whales. On the environmental side, the climate's warm regime of the 1980s and 1990s has had profound effects on gray whales and other marine life by shifting the distribution of feeding areas and prey populations on which the whales depend. On the other hand, warming of the seas and rising sea levels may foster new and expanded prey resources and territory for this species, as has occurred in the past. Further, should the climate cycle turn cool again, the perpetual challenges will once again confront all life.

Gray whales evolved over millions of years that witnessed drastic changes in sea level and the coastlines along which they roam. The modern gray whale we know today has endured thousands of years of changing ocean conditions, and is likely to survive both human and natural environmental perturbations, provided that human society recognizes it as a bonified co-habitant of the planet, and that we manage our own affairs accordingly.

EPILOGUE

White Ibis and Great Egrets take flight (with a Western Gull on the flats).

F AR FROM HOME, Laguna San Ignacio was to us an adventure beyond compare and rich with discovery. We sought to document what gray whales were do-ing each winter in Laguna San Ignacio. In the process we came to experience and understand the myriad of life that comprises this most unique of marine coastal ecosystems. It follows that we discovered much about ourselves too. Now some decades later, with this publication I've attempted to recount some of what we have learned and experienced in the process of those discoveries. I hope that the reader finds this account as interesting as the technical details, now well established in the scientific literature. If the visitor to Laguna San Ignacio finds the accounts and descriptions in this volume informative, and they enrich the visitor's experience and perception of the lagoon, I will have achieved my goal.

The government of Mexico has taken a leading role in the preservation of the gray whale. In 1972 it declared Laguna Ojo de Liebre (Scammon's Lagoon) as a refuge for gray whales-the first such sanctuary ever established in the world. In 1979, then President of Mexico, José Portillo, added Laguna San Ignacio to the list of gray whale refuges, further ensuring the gray whale's survival. The

Presidential Decree also established a permitting mechanism for scientific research and tourism in the area. It set aside specific areas for whale-watching, based in part on the findings of our research. It also placed the inner lagoon nursery off-limits to whale-watching tourism, and established the islands of the northern lagoon as bird sanctuaries. Finally Portillo's Decree re-defined the reserve at Ojo de Liebre (Scammon's) Lagoon and specifically included reserve status for Manuela and Guerrero Negro lagoons.

In 1988, President de la Madrid signed legislation creating the Vizcaíno Biosphere Reserve to encourage the conservation of endangered plant and animal species and permit only compatible human activities within its boundaries. The Biosphere Reserve included the gray whale breeding lagoons of Manuela, Guerrero Negro, Ojo de Liebre, and San Ignacio. It was gratifying to know that our studies at San Ignacio Lagoon contributed not only new knowledge on gray whale behavior and lagoon habitat use, but also insight into Mexico's conservation plan for the species. Mexico's commitment to the conservation of this unique area was re-affirmed by President Zedillio's decision in 2000 that the development of a solar salt production facility at the lagoon would be inconsistent with the mission of the Biosphere Reserve.

It is appropriate at this point to acknowledge our colleagues that shared our time at Laguna San Ignacio. There were a succession of field teams ranging from Mary Lou and myself in 1977, to upwards of twelve persons at times when we ran simultaneous abundance and distribution surveys. To those that endured the ups and downs of lagoon life with us we will be forever grateful, and they include: Mike "Eagle-Eye" Bursk; Gayle Dana; Mike Symons; James Sumich and his students; the owners and crews of the San Diego-based sportfishing fleet vessels *M/V Searcher*, *Spirit of Adventure*, *Qualifier 105*, *Mascot IV*, *Finalista 100*, *Pacific Queen*, and *Royal Polaris*; Peter Ott our naturalist "extrodinare"; Marylou, Shelly, Robbie and Bruce Mate; Marylyn and "Video" Bob Dahlheim; Louise Watson the "shell lady"; Janet Essley; Debbie and Dennis Miller who brought their Super Cub to the lagoon from Alaska; Jim Harvey and Mary Yockovich; and Howard Donner, AKA "El Sultán Número Dos."

Our sponsors and underwriters over the years included the San Diego Society of Natural History, the U.S. Marine Mammal Commission, the American Cetacean Society, the World Wildlife Fund, the National Geographic Society, Lindblad Expeditions, and the International Union for the Conservation of Nature (IUCN). Early advisors and mentors included Raymond Gilmore, Laura and Carl Hubbs. They eagerly opened their archives and offered opinions and advice on what we needed to do and how best to undertake our work. Dale Rice and Allen Wolman shared their experiences and knowledge of gray whales from their years of research. Michael Tillman and Howard Braham, both directors of the National Marine Fisheries Service's National Marine Mammal Laboratory, were always eager to assist by including our field program in the overall scientific efforts by their agency for gray whales. Equally supportive were John R. Twiss, Jr. and Robert J. Hofman of the U.S. Marine Mammal Commission. Permits to conduct our research were provided each year by the Mexican government, and the reports of our findings were utilized by Mexico to formulate their conservation measures for gray whales. Jorge Urbán R., Alejandro Gómez-Gallardo, and the student researchers from Mexico's universities were instrumental in resuming research and monitoring of gray whales in the lagoon during the 1990s. They contributed directly to the development and implementation of the Laguna San Ignacio Ecosystem Science Program in recent years. The resumption of scientific research in the lagoon was made possible by the generous commitments of The Ocean Foundation, the Pacific Life Foundation, World-Wildlife Fund of Mexico, and the Marisla Foundation.

I view the future for Laguna San Ignacio, its wildlife and its human residents, with great optimism. Conditions will continue to change as time passes, as they always do. There will be future challenges that will have to be addressed. Resources will cycle from times of plenty to periods of low abundance, driven by climatic uncertainty and the pressure of human utilization. The people and communities of Laguna San Ignacio are well on their way to their goal of establishing a sustainable lifestyle that does not threaten the integrity of the natural environment, the lagoon or its wildlife. Technologies are now available to deal with most of their day-to-day living needs. Undoubtedly, newer, better, and more eco-friendly technologies will become available in the future. Destructive over-consumption and outdated beliefs are giving way to more responsible and sustainable human behaviors. The success or failure of this enterprise will follow from the resolve of the local lagoon community and their dedication to set in motion trends and practices that will sustain a biologically robust environment, and to provide lifestyle options for their children and future generations.

As for La Laguna, well, as clearly demonstrated in my lifetime, she will always endure, provided we give her a chance. This endurance is truly the essence of "Lagoon Time."

My first touch in 1977.

PART II A Guide

Common Gray Whale Behaviors

L IKE ALL CETACEANS, gray whales spend the majority of their lives below the surface of the water and out of our view. Underwater, the visibility is limited and, unless a whale is very close, we cannot see much of what it is doing. However, as air breathing mammals they must come to the surface to breathe. This is the time the whales reveal much of their behavior to us. Gray whales in particular exhibit a variety of behaviors that may be seen at the surface in the breeding lagoons.

When surfacing to breathe, gray whales forcefully exhale. The "spout" or "blow" is a column of air mixed with water which appears bushy and "heart-shaped" when viewed from behind or ahead of the animal, or as a bushy column when seen from the side.

The typical gray whale columnar blow as viewed from the side (*above*), and the heart-shaped blow as viewed from behind (*right*). A stiff breeze will greatly affect the appearance of the blow. The intensity of the blow also changes with the whale's level of activity.

While migrating or swimming with purpose, gray whales frequently "throw" or "raise" their flukes above the surface of the water. This "fluking" behavior shown in the time series above usually marks the start of a "terminal dive" that follows a sequence of several respirations separated buy intervals of less than a minute before a longer, deeper dive lasing several minutes.

Perhaps the most spectacular behavior is the "breach" when a whale leaps above the surface, bringing its body out of the water to crash back again. Gray whales will often breach several times in sequence, forwards, backwards, or on its side, occasionally spinning a bit as they fall back into the water. The purpose for breaching has been debated over the years, but its specific purpose is not known. There are probably several reasons—shaking off parasites, to get higher above the surface for a look around, for communication, or perhaps just for fun. Because a whale may breach several times in row, the astute whale watcher will focus attention on the area of a breaching whale.

A more subdued breach of sorts is the "forward lunge" behavior that occurs when a whale lurches forward along the surface of the water while swimming at speed. Gray whales will frequently lunge at the surface while swimming fast or against the strong currents that are frequently encountered in the lagoons. By

surfacing this way they may reduce the drag or resistance of the water against their bodies as they swim. Frequently a calf will position itself alongside its mother when traveling fast, and appears to be "slipstreaming" as its mother lunges through the water's surface. This behavior is distinctly different from a feeding lunge.

A forward breach can be a behavior known as a "chin-slap." The key motion to notice that differentiates this behavior from a conventional breach is the whale's head. In a chin-slap, the whale will deliberately bend its head back, then move it down as to hit the surface with emphasis, making a bigger splash. Not all forward breaches are chin-slaps.

Scientists believe gray whales can see reasonably well through the air and will "spyhop" to have a look around or in the lagoons, to view passing boats. A whale displaying a full "spyhop" (*above left*) will slowly bring its head out of the water vertically, exposing the eyes above the surface, and then sink back below the surface. The key thing to observe is the eye looking back at you.

A similar behavior is the "head-out" or "head-raise" (*above right*) where the whale raises its snout out of the water, but does not expose its eyes. Often, the throat-pleats of "head-raising" whales are bulging or expanded, indicating that the whale has a mouth full of water and possibly bottom sediments. The distension happens quickly. Some believe the whales may be feeding during these events, but that depends on what's around to feed upon!

A whale on its side will watch what's on the surface. This behavior is the "gaze."

Using the other end of the body, gray whales may lift their tail flukes and tail vertically above the surface and waive them around for a few moments in what is referred to as tail-standing. Why they do this is anybody's guess!

Being buoyant in a water environment, whales do not need as much sleep as other mammals, but now and then they will rest at the surface, usually not for very long. This behavior is called "logging." Understandably, females with active calves are frequently observed taking these rests at or just below the surface. This behavior is also characterized by slow, relaxed blows with long intervals.

Common Winter Birds of Laguna San Ignacio

The assortment of birds that reside in or visit Laguna San Ignacio during the winter is diverse. The proximity of the lagoon to the open ocean and the mountain ranges of the Baja California peninsula provide opportunities for the visitor to view many oceanic and mainland species. Many species are year round residents of coastal Baja California that nest and reproduce there, while others are transient winter migrants that pass through the region or find the coastal lagoons of Baja California as their winter destinations. Enumerating the 430 or more species recorded for Baja California is an enormous undertaking, which we leave to the dedicated researchers that observe, describe, and document their presence on a continuing basis. Here we mention those birds that the winter visitor to the lagoon is most likely to observe, and that we and our colleagues have documented during the winter and early-spring months from January to April. We make no effort to be comprehensive in this regard. At the end of this section, there is a summary check list of common lagoon birds to assist the semi-serious birder with keeping track of what they encounter. For a more comprehensive inventory and background on the avifauna of the peninsula, we refer you to published guides such as *The Sibley Field Guide to Birds* by David Allen Sibley, Kenn Kaufman's *Guía de campo a la saves de Norteamérica*," and recent publications like Erickson et al. 2013 *Annotated Checklist of the Birds of Baja California and Baja California Sur, Second Edition* published in *North American Birds*. One may also obtain a working list of lagoon birds at our website www.lsiecosystem.org which is maintained by researchers that contribute to the Laguna San Ignacio Ecosystem Science Program.

Turkey Vulture

Osprey

The lagoon's proximity to the desert results in frequent sightings of birds that reside primarily in the mountains and mesas of the Baja California peninsula. Turkey vultures (*Cathartes aura*) are frequently seen soaring in the "thermals" of warm air rising out of the desert, and as carrion feeders they flock to feed on the decaying carcasses of whales, dolphins, and other animals that wash ashore within the lagoon. The abundant shore birds are preyed upon by Peregrine Falcons (*Falco peregrinus*), which find the remoteness of the lagoon suitable to their nesting and breeding habits. Other predatory birds seen near the lagoon include Kestrel or "Sparrow Hawks" (*Falco sparverius*), the Caracara (*Caracara cheriway*),

Black-chinned Sparrow

Ash-throated Flycatcher

Ravens

and the Loggerhead Shrike (*Lanius ludovicianus*) which has an interesting habit of impaling its prey on the thorns of desert cactus. Pairs of Ravens (*Crovus corax*) roam the desert shores of the lagoon looking for food and anything of interest, and readily adapt to human habitation. Working in pairs, they frequent the eco-tour camps and communities at Laguna San Ignacio where they boldly invade yards and homes, and will run off with anything of interest. They are capable of making a variety of unique sounds ranging from loud "caws" to guttural "gurgling" noises that seem odd coming from a bird. Both the Great Horned Owl (*Bubo virginianus*) and the Burrowing Owl (*Athene cunicularia*) may be encountered around the lagoon's desert shores where they prey on rodents in the nighttime hours. Burrowing owls nest and roost in abandoned animal burrows and are often seen perched along roadsides and desert shrubs. The soft gentile

Ruddy Turnstones

Peregrine Falcon

"cooing" of the Mourning Dove (*Zenaida macroura*) can be heard at daybreak and on calm evenings.

Laguna San Ignacio and much of the coastline are populated by Osprey "fish eagles" (*Pandion haliactus*) which thrive on the abundant fish found in the lagoon's waters. Osprey construct their nests in mid-winter, often returning to nesting sites from previous years. While they prefer to construct their nests on tall structures like clumps of desert cactus or brush, at Laguna San Ignacio they will often construct their nests on the ground especially on the small islands, or even on top of man-made structures such as power poles and buildings. Pairs of these birds will return year after year adding additional material to their nests until these piles of brush become substantial with some measuring a meter or more tall. The female may lay up to three eggs each season, and these hatch in March and April.

Eared Grebe

Short-billed Dowitcher

Common Egret

White Ibis

Both male and female will forage for fresh fish for themselves and their offspring. Competition between the chicks within the nest is extreme with usually only one chick surviving to fledge each year. In recent years artificial nesting platforms constructed from palm tree trunks and old power poles were erected along the southern shore of the lagoon, and within weeks of going up, each platform was occupied by a pair of nesting Osprey and continue to be used each winter.

The mangrove estuaries that thrive along much of the interior shores of the lagoon are the roosting and nesting sites for many of the wading bird species. The thick mangrove foliage provides a safe place to roost and avoid predators, and the numerous shallow pools formed at low tides in the waterways and channels are filled with small fish on which these birds feed. The largest include the Great Blue Heron (*Ardea Herodias*), the Common or Great Egret (*Ardea alba*), and the Tri-colored Heron (*Egretta tricolor*), all extremely spectacu-

Great Blue Heron

Reddish Egret

Yellow-crowned Night Heron

American Coot

lar in flight. Reddish egrets (*Egretta rufescens*) may be seen "dancing" around tide pools and flapping their wings to flush small fish out of their hiding places. Both the Black-crowned Night Heron (*Nycticorax nycticorax*) and the Yellow-crowned Night Heron (*Nycticorax violaceus*) reside in the mangrove thickets, along with, Little Blue Herons (*Egretta caerulea*) and Little Little Green Herons (*Butorides virescens*) that gather together to roost. Flocks of White Ibis (*Eudocimus albus*) and Snowy Egrets (*Egretta thula*) fly across the lagoon looking like dozens of flapping white handkerchiefs, and roost and forage in the mangroves among other wading birds.

More often heard rather than seen are the Clapper Rail (*Rallus longirostris*) and the Least Bittern (*Botaurus lentiginosus*). These secretive birds roam through the mangroves and stands of grasses along the tidal channels in search of prey, and their distinctive "clapping" or sharp "grunting" calls are very distinctive.

Tri-color Heron

Little Blue Heron

American Oystercatcher

Long-billed Curlew

Another easy to hear but hard to see bird is a small yellow warbler known as the Mangrove Warbler (*Dendroica* sp.). These warblers frequent the dense mangrove foliage where their characteristic yellow-green coloration blends with the green plants. They produce distinctive high pitched buzzing-like call accentuated with clear ascending and descending trills. Belted Kingfishers (*Ceryle alcyon*) are often seen perched atop the mangroves, and swooping down to pluck small fish from the tidal pools.

When the tides recede and expose the expansive sand and mudflats, the waders are joined by numerous species of shore birds that feast on the abundant invertebrate that are found in the sediments. Groups of Greater Yellowlegs (*Tringa melanoleuca*), Willets (*Catoptrophorus semipalmatus*), and Marbled Godwits (*Limosa fedoa*) move across the sandflats using their specialized elongate beaks to probe the sand for food. Other species that have migrated thousands of miles to winter

Marbled Godwits

Semi-palmated Sandpiper

at the lagoon include the Long-billed Curlew (*Numenius americanus*), Whimbrel (*Numenius phaeopus*), Willet (*Catoptrophorus semipalmatus*), Marbled Godwit (*Limosa fedoa*), and Avocetes (*Recurvirostra Americana*). Ruddy Turnstones (*Arenaria interpres*) and American Oystercatchers (*Haematopus palliates*) may be seen poking round the rocky shorelines for their prey. Other common shorebirds include Sandpipers, Plovers, Sanderlings, Dowitchers, Yellow Legs, and Phalaropes.

Wintertime migrants to Laguna San Ignacio include Brant (*Branta bernicla*), which gather by the hundreds in the lagoon's backwaters to forage on eelgrass (*Zostra marina*) in the shallows. Several ducks are regularly seen and include Red-breasted Mergansers (*Mergus serrator*), Common Goldeneye (*Bucephala clangula*), and Bufflehead (*Bucephala albeola*). Both the Pacific Loon (*Gavia pacifica*) and Common Loon (*Gavia immer*) move about the lagoon in search of fish.

Brant

Common Loon

Magnificent Frigatebird

As the tides fall and reveal sandy beaches on the shores of Laguna San Ig-nacio, a variety of shore and seabirds often form groups to sun themselves and await their next meal. Both adult and juvenile Brown Pelicans (*Pelecanus occidentalis*) are found in Laguna San Ignacio, gliding on the winds and diving head-first after fish. These birds nest on secluded islands and frequently sun themselves on the sand bars and shores of the lagoon at low tide. American White Pelicans (*Pelecanus erythrorhynchos*) soar over the lagoon in characteristic linear V-formation and find shelter from the winds in the quiet protected backwaters of the lagoon's mangrove channels and bays. It is twice as large as the Brown Pelican. While we have no evidence of them nesting at Laguna San Ignacio, Magnificent Frigatebirds (*Fregata magnificens*) occasionally fly over the lagoon, and will attack other seabirds in attempts to relieve them of any fish they have caught.

Double-crested Cormorant (*Phalacrocorax auritus*) and Brandt's Cormorant

White Pelican

Brown Pelican

Double-crested Cormorant

Surf Scoter (male)

(*Phalacrocorax penicillatus*) frequently form large floating rafts of hundreds of birds that follow and feed upon shoals of fish moving with the outgoing and incoming tides. Surf Scoters (*Melanitta perspicillata*), and Western Grebes (*Aechmophorus occidentalis*) are regular members of these floating communities. Parasitic Jaegers (*Stercoratius parasiticus*) are efficient pirates whose high speed chases of other birds often result in confrontations over fish. As the falling tides concentrate fish in the lagoon's channels, groups of Caspian Terns (*Sterna caspia*), Royal Terns (*Sterna maxima*), and Elegant Terns (*Sterna elegans*) fill the sky with their bright screams and calls as they plunge headward into the water after a fish meal. A number of distinctive gulls are present including magnificently colored Heermann's Gull (*Larus heermanni*), Western Gull (*Larus occidentalis*), and the Ring-billed Gull (*Larus delawarensis*). It is not unusual to observe a Western gull plucking a clam from the sand at low tide, taking it high into the air in its bill, and releasing the clam over a rocky area to have it break open, rewarding the clever bird with a fresh meal.

Heermann's gull

Royal Tern

List of Common Bird Species of Laguna San Ignacio

This list of common bird species does not include known vagrants. The reader is encouraged to consult a detailed field guide for all the birds. The English common name is followed by the local Spanish name and the taxonomic name.

Hummingbirds
TROCHILIDAE
    Costa's Hummingbird   Colibrí de Cabeza Violeta   *Calypte costae*

Loons
GAVIIDAE
    Common Loon   Colimbo Mayor   *Gavia immer*
    Pacific Loon   Colimbo Pacífico   *Gavia pacifica*

Grebes
PODICIPEDIDAE
    Western Grebe   Achichilique de Pico Amarillo   *Aechmophorus occidentalis*
    Eared Grebe   Zambullidor Orejudo   *Podiceps nigricollis*

Pelecaniformes
PELECANIDAE
    American White Pelican   Pelícano Blanco   *Pelecanus erythrorhynchos*
    Brown Pelican   Pelícano Pardo   *Pelecanus occidentalis*
FREGATIDAE
    Magnificent Frigatebird   Fragata Magnífica   *Fregata magnificens*
PHALACROCORACIDAE
    Double-crested Cormorant   Cormorán Orejudo   *Phalacrocorax auritus*
    Brandt's Cormorant   Cormorán de Brandt   *Phalacrocorax penicillatus*

Wading Birds
ARDEIDAE
    Great Blue Heron   Garzón Cenizo   *Ardea herodias*
    Great Egret   Garza Blanca   *Ardea alba*
    Snowy Egret   Garza de Dedos Dorados   *Egretta thula*
    Little Blue Heron   Garceta Azul   *Egretta caerulea*
    Green Heron   Garceta Verde   *Butorides virescens*
    Tricolored Heron   Garceta Tricolor   *Egretta tricolor*
    Reddish Egret   Garza Rojiza   *Egretta rufescens*
    Black-crowned Night-Heron   Pedrete de Corona Negra   *Nycticorax nycticorax*
    Yellow-crowned Night-Heron   Pedrette de Corona Clara   *Nyctanassa violacea*
    American Bittern   Avetoro Norteño   *Botaurus lentiginosus*
THRESKIORNITHIDAE
    White Ibis   Ibis Blanco   *Eudocimus albus*

Geese and Ducks

ANATIDAE

Surf Scoter	Negreta de Nuca Blanca	*Melanitta perspicillata*
Red-Brested Merganser	Mergo Copetón	*Mergus serrator*
Bufflehead	Pato Monja	*Bucephala albeola*
Ruddy Duck	Pato Tepalcate	*Oxyura jamaicensis*
Brant	Ganso de Collar	*Branta bernicla*

Diurnal Raptors

ACCIPITRIDAE

Osprey	Gavilán Pescador	*Pandion haliaetus*

CATHARTIDAE

Turkey Vulture	Zopilote Aura	*Cathartes aura*

FALCONIDAE

Peregrine Falcon	Halcón Peregrino	*Falco peregrinus*

Gruiformes

RALLIDAE

American Coot	Fulica americana	*Fulica americana*

Shorebirds

CHARADRIIDAE

Killdeer	Chorlo Tildío	*Charadrius vociferus*
Semipalmated Plover	Chorlito Semipalmeado	*Charadrius semipalmatus*
Snowy Plover	Chorlito Nevado	*Charadrius alexandrinus*
Black-bellied Plover	Chorlo Gris	*Pluvialis squatarola*

RECURVIROSTRIDAE

Black-necked Stilt	Candelero Americano	*Himantopus mexicanus*
American Avocet	Avdceta Americana	*Recurvirostra americana*

HAEMATOPODIDAE

American Oystercatcher	Ostrero Americano	*Haematopus palliatus*
Black Oystercatcher	Ostrero Negro	*Haematopus bachmani*

SCOLOPACIDAE

Dunlin	Playero de Dorso Rojo	*Calidris alpina*
Least Sandpiper	Playerito Chichicuilote	*Calidris minutilla*
Western Sandpiper	Playero Occidental	*Calidris mauri*
Ruddy Turnstone	Vuelvepiedras Rojizo	*Arenaria interpres*
Black Turnstone	Vuelvepiedras Negro	*Arenaria melanocephala*
Lesser Yellowlegs	Patamarilla Menor	*Tringa flavipes*
Greater Yellowlegs	Patamarilla Mayor	*Tringa melanoleuca*
Long-billed Dowitcher	Costurero de Pico Largo	*Limnodromus scolopaceus*
Short-billed Dowitcher	Costurero de Pico Corto	*Limnodromus griseus*
Willet	Playero Pihuihui	*Catoptrophorus semipalmatus*
Marbled Godwit	Picopando Canelo	*Limosa fedoa*
Wimbrel	Zarapito Trinador	*Numenius phaeopus*
Long-billed Curlew	Zarapito Picolargo	*Numenius americanus*

Gulls, Terns, Skimmers, Jaegers, and Skuas

LARIDAE
Ring-billed Gull	Gaviota de Pico Anillado	*Larus delawarensis*
Western Gull	Gaviota Occidental	*Larus occidentalis*
Heermann's Gull	Gaviota Ploma	*Larus heermanni*
Forster's Tern	Charrán de Forster	*Sterna forsteri*
Caspian Tern	Charrán Caspia	*Sterna caspia*
Royal Tern	Charrán Real	*Sterna maxima*
Elegant Tern	Charran Elegante	*Sterna elegans*
Pomarine Jaeger	Salteador Pomarino	*Stercorarius Pomarinus*

Pigeons and Doves

COLUMBIDAE
White-winged Dove	Paloma de Ala Blanca	*Zenaida asistica*

Kingfishers

ALCEDINIDAE
Belted Kingfisher	Martín Pescador Norteño	*Ceryle alcyon*

Shrikes and Vireos

LANIIDAE
Loggerhead Shrike	Alcaudóon Verdugo	*Lanius ludovicianus*

Crows and Ravens

CORVIDAE
Common Raven	Cuervo Común	*Corvus corax*

Larks

ALAUDIDAE
Horned Lark	Alondra Cornuda	*Eremophila alpestris*

Warblers

PARULIDAE
Mangrove Warbler	Chipe de Mangle	*Dendroica* sp.

Sparrows

PASSERIDAE
Savannah Sparrow	Gorrión Sabanero	*Passerculus sandwichensis*
Black-throated Sparrow	Gorrión de Garganta Negra	*Amphispiza bilineata*

Wrens

TROGLODYTIDAE
Cactus Wren	Matraca Del Desierto	*Campylorhynchus brunneicapillus*

Common Mammals of Laguna San Ignacio

In addition to gray whales, Laguna San Ignacio is home to a variety of marine and terrestrial mammals that are permanent residents or reside in the lagoon watershed or the lagoon itself.

Along with gray whales, groups of bottlenose dolphin (*Tursiops truncatus*) roam the lagoon interior during the winter months. The local fishermen tell us that bottlenose dolphins may be encountered during all months of the year, and they frequently will race to intercept moving boats to briefly "bow ride" on the pressure wake of the boats. Groups of these dolphin follow schools of fish that move with the falling tides that spill across the sandflats. It is not unusual to see one or more bottlenose dolphins tossing a larger fish around at the surface of the water, or playfully leaping out of the water, but just why they do this is not clear. Over the winters we've opportunistically photographed many individual bottlenose dolphin in Laguna San Ignacio and learned to recognize several individuals by the white scars on their flanks and cuts and nicks in their dorsal fins.

California sea lions (*Zalophus californicanus*) haul-out on the outer beaches of the barrier islands that protect the lagoon interior from surf and storms. In winter groups of 50 or more animals will haul up onto the beach above the high tide

line to bask in the sun. Local naturalist and fisherman Ranulfo Mayoral noticed that during the summer months groups of male and a few females California sea lions will gather and haul-out on the southern end of Isla Pelicanos within the lagoon during the summer months. During October and November, Ranulfo observes upwards of 150 California sea lions, mostly bachelor males and a few females. He has not seen any evidence of pups being born in these groups.

The desert around the lagoon and its shores are routinely patrolled by coy-

otes (*Canis latrans*) looking for carrion and to ambush marine birds along the shorelines. Some individuals have learned to dig for clams and hatchet scallops that are visible on the sandflats when exposed at low tides. In recent years coyotes have made their way onto the sand and barrier islands in the lagoon basin, and this has had a devastating impact on many of the ground nesting birds, like the Osprey, pelicans, cormorants, and egrets. As more and more humans visit the lagoon, the coyotes are becoming bolder and are frequently seen prowling through the eco-tour camps during the days. At night, groups of coyotes in different locations will exchange "choruses" of their distinctive howls throughout the night.

Deer Mouse, *Peromyscus maniculatus*.
Photo: Sergio Martinez

Kangaroo Rat, *Dipodomys merriami*.
Photo: Gerardo Cebalolos

A common desert mammal, especially around human habitation, is the Deer mouse (*Peromyscus maniculatus*) and its cousin the Kangroo Rat (*Dipodomys* sp.). These small rodents forage during the nighttime hours for seeds, small insects, plants, and if they can find it, bits of food left over from humans that reside at the lagoon. The distinctive long tail of the K rat sets it apart from the smaller Deer mouse. Deer mice are known to carry the infectious "Hantavirus" which is contagious to humans if they come into contact with the animal's droppings, urine or saliva.

The largest desert mammal to frequent the Laguna San Ignacio area is seldom seen, but leaves its footprints in the sandflats and salt marshes around the northern shores of the lagoon. The native, but endangered Pronghorned antelope, or Berrendo (*Antilocapra americana peninsularis*), is a subspecies of the North American antelope endemic to Baja California. For many decades these animals were found only in the desert south of Laguna Ojo de Liebre and in the

"Berenndo" (*Antilocapra americana peninsularis*), an endangered subspecies of the North American Antelope resides within the Vizcaíno Desert. Photo: Sergio Martinez

Santa Clara mountains. Conservation efforts to protect the small herds from poachers, and a captive breeding program have encouraged the recovery of the species in Baja California. We frequently find fresh foot-prints of these antelope in the salt flats and tidal areas along the northern shores of the Laguna San Ignacio, but we have yet to see an individual. Apparently as this elusive species' numbers are increasing, they are beginning to re-occupy their former range throughout the Vizcaíno desert of Baja California and within the Biosphere Reserve.

Donkeys (*Equus africanus asinus*), a domesticated member of the Equidae or horse family were introduced to Baja California during colonial times to serve as work animals, as were mules which are hybrid equids resulting from the cross breeding of a female horse and a male donkey. These animals are known for their ability to transport people and goods over rugged terrain. As one would expect, some of these animals escaped from captivity and have roamed the deserts of Baja California, and occasionally they are seen along the roads or where water is reliably found.

The desert surrounding Laguna San Ignacio is the home of the black-tailed jackrabbit (*Lepus californicus*). This large brown to grey hare does not dig burrows, but prefers to find depressions under trees to avoid predators. Its ears are longer than hits hind legs. It has a black stripe on the back of the tail and a spot at the tip of both ears. It is rarely seen during the day unless surprised and flushed from its hiding places. They are most often seen at dusk and in the early morning when they forage on plant leaves and other vegetation. Brush rabbits are important food for coyotes and bobcats.

Photo: Gerardo Ceballos.

List of Common Mammals of Laguna San Ignacio

CETACEA
    Gray Whale   Ballena gris   *Eschrichtius robustus*
    Bottlenose Dolphin   Delfin mular   *Tursiops truncatus*

PINNIPEDIA
    California Sea Lion   Lobo del Mar   *Zalophus californicanus*

CANINIDAE
    Coyote   Coyote   *Canis latrans*

RODENTIA
    Deer Mouse   Ratón ciervo   *Paramiscous maniculatus*
    Kangaroo Rat   Ratón canguro *Dipodomys* sp.

UNGULATA
    Pronghorned Antelope Berrendo   *Antilocapra americana peninsularis*
    Donkeys   Burro   *Equus africanus asinus*

LAGOMORPHA
    Black-tailed Jack Rabbit Liebre   *Lepus californicus*

Common Desert and Lagoon Plants

L AGUNA SAN IGNACIO lies within and is part of the greater Vizcaíno desert. The abundance, diversity and distribution of trees, shrubs, and other plants that occur in the region of the lagoon are determined by a number of physical and climatic features characteristic of the desert and its interface with the coastal ocean.

The region receives less than a centimeter of rain each year, yet the plant life thrives on fresh water from fogs, that can blanket the coastal region. The proximity to the cold Pacific water and warm desert inland air result in frequent coastal throughout the year. Fresh water condenses from these fogs, providing life giving water for plants and animals alike. Relentless northerly and north-westerly winds constrain vertical growth to only the most durable plants and trees, and the growth of the less sturdy species tends to produce low lying and often contorted individuals.

The diversity of plant life at the lagoon is a mix of characteristic desert species, and those that are able to tolerate the alkaline and saline conditions of the coastal plains and saltflats, intertidal mudflats, and the nutrient poor clays and sandstone soils surrounding the lagoon's shores. A visitor's first impression of the lagoon's desert's flora is often of a dry, grey-brown, desiccated landscape, void of any tall trees and dominated by low scrub brush and cactus. Closer examination reveals a vast diversity of plants of many and varied shapes and designs, all specially adapted to the specific physical characteristics of the desert-marine environment.

Cardón Cactus Patch with Cholla and an Osprey

Cardón Cactus Forest

If the visitor arrives within a few weeks following a substantial rain, they may be treated to a colorful and fragrant mix of flowering plants and green shrubbery. Many of the lagoon's plants respond quickly to the periodic rainfall by flowering and sprouting leaves to take advantage of these short-lived opportunities to grow, produce leaves and seed. Green leaves photosynthesize sugars which are quickly converted into flowers and seeds before the moisture is gone. Once dry conditions again prevail, green leaves yellow and drop from the plants. Flowers wilt and the winds disburse their seeds to await the next rain event. These periodic explosions of flowers may occur years apart, and when they occur, the lagoon's plant life capitalizes on these moments for reproduction.

Other plants have evolved special adaptations to utilize the more reliable marine water source that comes with each changing of the tides. Salt water tolerant, or "halophytic" plants, thrive in salty water by extracting the water necessary for life, and concentrating and even excreting salt that would otherwise prevent their existence. The shorelines and margins of the lagoon-sea interface are densely populated with communities of these salt tolerant plants. Such areas develop extensive mangrove lined estuaries and vast tidal marshlands, which in turn provide habitat and food for many of the lagoon's marine and terrestrial species.

Here we provide an overview of some the most common and evident plants the visitor to the lagoon will encounter and likely observe at Laguna San Ignacio. For a more comprehensive and detailed description of the plants of Baja California's lagoon regions, we refer the visitor to the *Baja California Plant Field Guide, 3rd Edition* by Jon P. Rebman and Norman C. Roberts.

Desert Plants

By far the most predominant and largest of the desert plants found at Laguna San Ignacio is the Elephant or Cardón cactus (*Pachycereus pringlei*). These long-lived giants may be found in dense stands or "forests" throughout the Vizcaíno Desert region. These cactus are the tallest plants in the lagoon's skyline, with some reaching 20 m tall with several lateral arms or branches, and living for hundreds of years. This species specializes is storing water in its tissues, with its ribbed or pleated stems swelling during periods of rain and contracting during droughts. The interior of the plant contains woody rods which form a stout skeleton, and are used as building materials by local people. White flowers appear from April to June and produce a fleshy round fruit full of seeds which are dispersed by birds and mammals that rely on the fruit as an important food source.

The next tallest plant at the lagoon is the Baja California Yucca (*Yucca valida*) reaching 3–7 m, growing in clumps or clusters, often branched, twisted and contorted by the prevailing lagoon winds. The Baja Yucca or "Datilillo" is endemic to Baja California provides habitat for nesting birds in its arms. Its creamy-white flowers produce oblong fleshy sweet fruit which may be used to make a tea or eaten. The fibers of the plant may be used as building materials, and ranchers use the trunks of the plant as fence posts, which then sprout to produce living fences around their homes.

Elephant Trees (*Bursera* sp.) with their characteristic thick trunks and limbs, and peeling paper-like bark are found in the desert to the east of the lagoon. Like other desert plants these trees are adapted to store and conserve water is

Yucca

Elephant Tree

their thick tissues. Most of the year their branches are naked, but soon after any rainfall, they sprout delicate pinnately compound leaves to capture the sunlight. The relentless desert winds cause many Elephant trees to produce sprawling, twisted, and contorted prostrate branches.

Another predominant member of the lagoon's flora is Adam's Tree or Palo Adán (*Fouquieria diguetii*). This member of the Ocotillo family is related to the Boojum Tree (*Fouquieria columnaris*) of the Central Baja Peninsula, and the Ocotillo or "Coachwhip" (*Fouquieria splendens*). Unlike the Boojum or Ocotillo, the Palo Adán develops a thick short trunk at its base from which multiple branched limbs develop. It produces multiple small green leaves and bright red clusters of flowers which are pollinated by humming birds.

Palo Adán

Lomboy

The Lomboy (*Jatropha cinerea*) is a small treelike shrub with thick trunks and flexible branches. Mostly naked during the year, the Lomboy responds quickly to rainfall by producing dark green, waxy ovate leaves. If no more rain falls, the leaves quickly turn yellow and are shed to conserve moisture. Lomboy's produce small pinkish flowers and small green fruit containing seeds.

Additional cactus found in the desert surrounding the lagoon include the

Old Man Cactus

Galloping Cactus (*Stenocereus gummosus*), the bearded Old Man Cactus or "Garambullo" (*Lophocereus schottii*), several species of "jumping cactus" or Chollas (*Cylindropuntia* sp.), the Fishhook Cactus (*Mammillaria* sp.) and small specimens of Barrel Cactus (*Ferocactus* sp.). Due to a lack of traditional "trees," many desert and lagoon birds utilize the larger cactus as foundations for their nests, often building extensive platforms of twigs and sticks within the cactus' spiny branches.

Alkaline Plains

Freshwater is an infrequent commodity in the desert surrounding Laguna San Ignacio. The soil is an alkaline mixture of fine clays, sand, limestone shells, and alluvial rocks and pebbles left over from centuries of erosion from wind and water. Most moisture comes from coastal fog, dewfall, and scarce amounts of rainfall during the year. The soils are hydrophilic and soak up whatever moisture is available. In doing so the soil will swell-up like rising bread, and once the sun dries the surface, a crust of alkaline soil forms and "crunches" underfoot. Morning fogs also encourage the growth of the epiphytic bromeliads like Veatch Dodder (*Cuscuta veatchii*) whose bright orange tendrils climb and often cover desert plants.

If sufficient rainfall occurs, the desert comes alive with green shrubs and multicolored flowers, providing a brief but fragrant floral display. Quick to respond to the rain are the bright blue Palmer Sand Lily (*Triteleiopsis palmeri*) perched on high stalks, the delicate White-Hair Cryptantha (*Cryptantha maritime*), blue Lupine (*Lupinus* sp.), yellow Brittlebush (*Encelia farinosa*) and California Trixis (*Trixis californica*). Rock Daisy (*Amauria rotundifolia*) may form carpets across the sandy soils, along with yellow Suncup (*Camissonia angelorum*), and the orange Mallow (*Abutilon palmeri*).

Other dominant shrubs found in the extensive alkaline plains around lagoon include the Cliff Spurge (*Euphorbia misera*) with its delicate pinkish flowers, Saltbush (*Atriplex julacea*), Saltbush (*Atriplex* sp.), the Iodine Bush (*Allenrolfea occidentalis*), and the California Desert Thorn (*Lycium californicum*) with its bright red berries.

Intertidal Margin

Intertidal Margins

As it approaches the lagoon shores, the desert transitions into extensive tidal flood plains and salt marshes. This is the habitat of salt-tolerant "halophytes" that are adapted to thrive on seawater brought to the shores with each rising tide. Plants found here are able to withstand periodic submergence in seawater flooding over the sand flats and into portions of the desert. Rimming intertidal flats are often found a mix of Palmer Frankennia (*Frankenia plameri*), Iodine Bush (*Allenrolfea occidentalis*) Pickleweed (*Salicornia* sp.), Saltwort (*Batis maritima*), and saltbush (*Atriplex* sp.). Closer to the sand flats are stands of Cordgrass (*Spartina foliosa*), and Saltgrass (*Distichlis spicata*) often thrive.

The region immediately around Laguna San Ignacio represents the northernmost range of the mangroves along the Pacific coast of Baja California. These plants form dense thickets 4–6 m tall around the margins of the lagoon where tidal waters reach into the desert. There are three mangrove families represented at Laguna San Ignacio: these are the Red Mangrove (*Rhizophora mangle*), White Mangrove (*Laguncularia racemosa*), and the Black Mangrove (*Avicennia germinans*).

The Red and White Mangroves frequently grow together and form extensive networks of impenetrable prop roots topped by dense green foliage. A brightly colored green spider with sharply pointed red projections from its body is found within the leaves of the mangroves. A small "tree oyster" lives on the surface of these prop roots, and the network of channels formed by the interlacing prop roots is habitat for juvenile fish. The Red Mangrove bears white and yellow flowers which germinate while attached to the plant. From these grow elongated club-shaped "pod-like" seedlings that may reach 20 cm long. These seedlings fall from the plants and will float in seawater allowing the outgoing tides to disburse them throughout the lagoon and along the coast. If they wash ashore in a suitable location, the seedlings will root and grow into new Red Mangrove plants.

The Black Mangrove form a thick trunk at its base from which branched limbs grow vertically, and are covered with long, evergreen, elliptic-ovate leaves. The leaves can concentrate and excrete salt from specialized glands. Each Black Mangrove plant extends networks of widely spread cable roots under the thick sandy and muddy sediments. At regular intervals along these roots lobe-like "pneumatophores" emerge from the sediments and are bathed by the rising and falling tides, allowing for nutrient and oxygen exchange with the tidal water. Like other mangroves, the Black Mangrove produces seeds that germinate while on the plant, then fall and will float in seawater to be disbursed by the tides.

Where sand dunes form barriers to the sea several succulent-like plants sprawl out over the surface of the sand and thereby stabilize the sand. These include Red Sand-Verbena (*Abronia maritima*), White-Leaf Spurge (*Euphorbia leucophylla*), Sea-Pursiana (*Sesvium verrucosum*), and Salt Wart (*Batis maritima*). The non-native Crystalline iceplant (*Mesembryanthemum crystallinum*) grows here as well as along roads and in disturbed areas surrounding the lagoon.

Succlent-like plants frequently carpet the intertidal margins along the shoreline of the lagoon's marshes.

List of Common Plants of Laguna San Ignacio

Succulents

Elephant Cactus	Cardón	*Pachycereus pringlei*
Baja California Yucca	Datilillo	*Yucca valida*
Elephant Tree	Torote	*Bursera* sp.
Adam's Tree	Palo Adán	*Fouquieria diguetii*
Lomboy or Ashy Limberbush	Sangrengado	*Jatropha cinerea*
Galloping Cactus	Pitaya Agria	*Stenocereus gummosus*
Old Man Cactus	Garambullo	*Lophocereus schottii*
Chollas	Cholla	*Cylindropuntia* sp.
California Fishhook Cactus	Biznaguita	*Mammillaria* sp.
Barrel Cactus	Biznaga	*Ferocactus* sp.

Alkaline Plains

Cliff Spurge	Jumetón / Tacora	*Euphorbia misera*
Palmer Frankenia	Yerba Reuma	*Frankenia plameri*
Vizcaíno Saltbush	Chamizo	*Atriplex julacea*
Iodine Bush	Chamizo	*Allenrolfea occidentalis*
Desert Thorn	Frutilla / Salicieso	*Lycium californicum*
Veatch Dodder	Manto de la Virgin	*Cuscuta veatchii*

Flowers

Palmer Sand Lily	Coveria	*Triteleiopsis palmeri*
White-Hair Cryptantha	Crypantha	*Cryptantha maritime*
Blue Lupine	Lupino / Garbancillo	*Lupinus* sp.
Brittlebush	Incienso	*Encelia farinosa*
California Trixis	Plumilla / Santa Lucia	*Trixis californica*
Rock Daisy	Manzanillo	*Amauria rotundifolia*
Suncup	Camissonia	*Camissonia angelorum*
Mallow	Mallow	*Abutilon palmeri*

Intertidal Margins

Pickleweed	Salicornia	*Salicornia* sp.
Saltwort	Dedito	*Batis maritima*
Cordgrass	Spartina	*Spartina foliosa*
Saltgrass	Distichlis	*Distichlis spicata*
Red Mangrove	Mangle Rojo	*Rhizophora mangle*
White Mangrove	Mangle Blanco	*Laguncularia racemosa*
Black Mangrove	Mangle Negro	*Avicennia germinans*

Dunes Plants

Red Sand-Verbena	Alfombrilla	*Abronia maritima*
White-Leaf Spurge	Golondrina	*Euphorbia leucophylla*
Sea-Pursiane	Cenicilla / Saladilla	*Sesvium verrucosum*
Crystalline Iceplant	Vidriero / Hielito	*Mesembryanthemum crystallinum*

References and Resources

Berta, A., Sumich, J.L. and Kovacs, K.M. 2006. Marine Mammals: Evolutionary Biology, 2nd Edition. Elsevier-Academic Press, New York. 547 pp.

Ceballos, G., ed. 2014. Mammals of Mexico, English Edition. Johns Hopkins University Press. 992 pp.

Crosby, H.W. 1984. The Cave Paintings of Baja California, Revised Edition. Copley Books, San Diego. 189 pp.

Dedina, S. 2000. Saving the Gray Whale: People, Politics, and Conservation in Baja California. University of Arizona Press, Tucson. 186 pp.

Erickson, R.A., Carmona, R., Ruiz-Campos, G., Iliff, M.J., and Billings, M.J. 2013. Annotated Checklist of the Birds of Baja California and Baja California Sur, Second Edition. North American Birds, 66(4). 582-613 pp.

Folkens, P.A., Reeves, R.R., Stewart, B.S., Clapham, P.J., and Powell, J.A. 2002. National Audubon Society Guide to Marine Mammals of the World. Alfred A. Knoff, New York. 527 pp.

Jones, M.L., Swartz, S.L., and Leatherwood, S. (eds). 1984. The Gray Whale, *Eschrichtius robustus*. Academic Press, Inc., Orlando. 600 pp.

Jones, M.L. and Swartz, S.L. 2009. "Gray Whale, *Eschrichtius robustus*." pp. 503–511 in: Perrin, W.F., Wursig, B., and Thewissen, J.G.M. (eds): Encyclopedia of Marine Mammals, Second Edition. Elsevier-Academic Press, Inc., New York, NY.

Kaufman, K. 2005. Guia de Campo a las Aves de Norteamerica. Houghton Miffin Co., New York, New York. 391 pp.

Landauer, L.B. 1986. Scammon: Beyond the Lagoon, A Biography of Charles Melville Scammon. Flying Cloud Press, Pasadena, California. 180 pp.

Laylander, D. and Moore, J.D., (eds). 2006 "The Prehistory of Baja California: Advances in the Archaeology of the Forgotten Peninsula." University Press of Florida, Gainesville.

Rebman, J.P. and Roberts, N.C. 2012. Baja California Plant and Field Guide, 3rd Edition. San Diego Natural History Museum, Sun Belt Publications, San Diego. 451 pp.

Russell, D. 2001. Eye of the Whale: Epic Passage from Baja to Siberia. Simon and Schuster, New York. 688 pp.

Scammon, C. M. 1874. The Marine Mammals of the Northwestern Coast of North America, Together with an Account of the American Whale Fishery. Reprinted in: 1968 by Dover Publications, Inc., New York. 319 pp.

Sibley, D.A. 2000. The Sibley Guide to Birds. Alfred A. Knopf, Inc., New York. 544 pp.

Internet Resources

Baja Discovery Eco-Tours: www.bajadiscovery.com

Baja Expeditions Eco-Tours: www.bajaex.com

International Community Foundation: www.icfdn.org

International Union for the Conservation of Nature: www.iucn.org

International Whaling Commission, Scientific Committee: www.iwc.int

Kuyma Eco-Tourism: www.kuyima.com

Laguna San Ignacio Ecosystem Science Program: www.lsiecosystem.org

M/V Searcher Natural History Tours: www.bajawhale.com

Natural Resources Defense Council: www.nrdc.org

Pachico's Whalewatching: www.pachicosecotours.com

Pronatura- Noroeste: www.pronatura-noroeste.org

The Ocean Foundation: www.oceanfdn.org

SEMARNAT: www.semarnat.gob.mx

Spirit of Adventure Charters: www.spiritofadventurefishing.com

WildCoast: www.wildcoast.net

World Wildlife Fund: www.worldwildlife.org

Caudal peduncle
(tail muscle)